How to Select and Manage Consultants

How to Select and Manage Consultants

A Guide to Getting What You Pay For

Howard L. Shenson, CMC

Lexington Books
D.C. Heath and Company/Lexington, Massachusetts/Toronto

———————————— in association with ————————————

University Associates, Inc.
San Diego, California

Library of Congress Cataloging-in-Publication Data

Shenson, Howard L.
How to select and manage consultants / Howard L. Shenson
p.   cm.
Includes bibliographical references.
ISBN 0–669–21129–X (alk. paper)
1. Consultants. 2. Consultants—Selection and appointment.
3. Consultants—United States—Selection and appointment.
I. Title.
HD69.C6S5175   1990
658.4'6—dc20   89–35306
CIP

Published simultaneously in Canada
Printed in the United States of America
Casebound International Standard Book Number: 0–669–21129–X
Library of Congress Catalog Card Number: 89–35306

The paper used in this publication meets
the minimum requirements of American National Standard
for Information Sciences—Permanence of Paper
for Printed Library Materials, ANSI Z39.48–1948.

90 91 92 8 7 6 5 4 3 2 1

To Joanie, David, Jon, and Brian

Contents

viii

Preface

C onsulting—the giving of advice and rendering of opinion—
is considered by many to be the world's second oldest profession. The desire to tell others what to do and how to do it has
always been irresistible. To do so for a fee has been particularly
intriguing and attractive. Despite its longevity and attraction,
however, consulting has remained a little-noticed, sleepy profession for almost its entire history.

Although the ranks of consultants have increased slowly and
consistently since the birth of the Industrial Revolution, it was
not until the late 1960s and 1970s that growth became pro-
nounced. Widespread and pervasive changes in the society and
economy, particularly acute in the United States, caused the
number of consultants to grow spectacularly. In the United
States, the number has grown from roughly sixty thousand in
1960 to more than four hundred thousand in the late 1980s. The
increase of course, resulted from an increasing demand for their
services.

But unlike other professions, the demand was often generated
by the consultants themselves. It was they who decided on the
independent, entrepreneurial lifestyle first. Once the decision and
commitment was made, the necessity of selling their specific services, as well as educating the client market about the wisdom of
retaining a consultant, fell upon their shoulders. They did a
remarkably good job. Consultants saw their incomes grow at a
rate of more than double the cost of living in the 1970s.

This book is designed to assist the client (corporate, governmental, institutional, and individual) with understanding, select-

ing, compensating, managing, and evaluating consultants. Because many decision-makers are inexperienced in working with consultants and because opportunities to use consultants are growing, it is hoped the reader will find answers to questions about consulting, the consulting process, and the client-consultant relationship, as well as identify potential, profitable uses for consultants and other professional practitioners.

If you are not now using consultants in the planning or execution of your daily affairs, it is increasingly likely that you will be in the months or years immediately ahead. The pace of technological change, the complexity and growing competitiveness of the economy, increasing regulations, and the growing importance of knowledge and information (relative to capital) for business and organizational success will likely compel you to seek outside "experts," "authorities," or "specialists." The identification, evaluation, selection, and management of such outside consultants is something with which most managers and executives have little familiarity and great uncertainty. This book is designed to shorten your learning curve and allow you to obtain better outside assistance and to do so at lower cost and for greater benefit or results.

Acknowledgment

I would like to thank Tiffany Jordan for her creative and exacting editing of the manuscript.

Introduction

I f you think you might benefit from a consultant's services, or if you already know you need a consultant and are looking for one, or if you just would like to know a little more about what consultants do and how clients use them, then this book should help. It provides information about finding, retaining, working with, evaluating, and making the most of consultants.

Chapter 1 defines and describes in general terms what a consultant is and does. This chapter includes information about:

1. The definition of a consultant
2. The need and demand for consultants
3. Services and activities of consultants
4. Qualities of consultants

Chapter 2 illustrates the differing roles of the consultant and some of the reasons why clients use consultants. Included are descriptions of ten situations in which a consultant's services are often needed:

1. The need for specialized expertise, talent, or skill
2. The need for an independent, unbiased, frank opinion
3. The need for temporary technical assistance
4. Business cash flow problems
5. The need for expertise in acquiring resources
6. Political/Organizational problems
7. Regulation
8. Availability of funds

9. Saving key personnel
10. Training

In chapter 3, you will find information about and comparisons of the different types of consultants and a checklist of questions to help you determine what sort of consultant might benefit you the most. Types of consultants consist of the following:

1. Operational vs. advisory
2. Part-time vs. full-time
3. Process vs. functional
4. Large firm vs. small firm
5. Academic vs. commercial

Chapter 4 provides a brief overview of the consulting process from beginning (the consultant's marketing and public relations) to end (the reporting and evaluation).

Chapter 5 offers ways a client can find qualified consultants:

1. Define needs and objectives
2. Consultants come to you
3. Referrals
4. Reading/Writing ads
5. Directories
6. Research for the ideal consultant
7. Leading authorities
8. Trade and professional associations
9. Brokers

In chapter 6, you will find information about interviewing and evaluating potential consultants. Included is information about:

1. The first meeting between client and potential consultant

2. Questions to ask a consultant (and yourself) to evaluate a consultant's skills

3. Discussing outcomes and expectations

4. Establishing measurable objectives

5. Discussing business arrangements

6. Checking a consultant's experience and references

7. Client fears

8. Consultant fears

9. Consultant's marketing

Chapter 7 provides information about the consultant's fee. Included are the following:

1. Median daily billing rate for consultants, by specialty

2. Median annual income for consultants according to specialty

3. Breakdown of the daily billing rate and analysis of its components

4. Cost comparison between consultant and staff member

Chapter 8 reveals how consultants determine their overhead, providing an example consultant and breaking down his overhead into its expense categories.

Chapter 9 covers fee disclosure by the consultant. It also describes various types of fees and contracts and their risks and advantages:

1. Daily/hourly fee

2. Fixed-price fee: firm fixed-price, fixed-fee-plus-expenses, escalating fixed-price, incentive fixed-price, performance fixed-price, fixed-price with redetermination

3. Time-and-material contracts

4. Cost reimbursement contracts: cost contract, cost-plus-fixed-fee, cost-plus-incentive-fee, cost-plus-award-fee

5. Retainer contracts

6. Performance/Contingency contracts

Chapter 10 contains information about the proposal and its components and includes two sample proposals—a letter proposal and a combined proposal/contract.

Chapter 11 outlines aspects of the contract and provides sample contracts for the reader to examine.

In chapter 12 you will find ways clients get free consulting through:

1. Proposal writing
2. Follow-up
3. Diagnosis/Needs analysis
4. Future riches
5. Diversion

Chapter 13 illustrates ways consultants refuse a job or turn an assignment around to their advantage:

1. "I don't do that."
2. "I'm too busy."
3. Redefinition
4. High bid
5. Conflict of interest
6. A piece of the assignment

Chapter 14 describes ways to enhance the client-consultant relationship and to make it run smoothly, as well as suggests ways a client can manage a consultant effectively. This chapter provides a sample progress report and a checklist of questions for the client to use to evaluate his or her management effectiveness and includes information about:

1. Setting precise objectives
2. Establishing observable milestones
3. Working with a written contract
4. Requiring progress reports
5. Establishing open communications

6. Appointing a staff member as a liaison
7. Scheduling phased payments
8. Creating a supportive environment
9. Providing quick feedback

Chapter 15 describes ten potential problem areas—ten issues clients and consultants should discuss before the consultation:

1. Conflict of interests
2. Creative outcomes
3. Associates and subcontractors
4. Time management
5. Insurance/liability
6. Termination
7. Nonperformance
8. Arbitration
9. Expenses
10. Confidentiality

Chapter 16 provides information about evaluating the consultation. A final report can be an essential part of evaluation; thus, this chapter describes components of, requisites for, and benefits of the written final report. This chapter also suggests a few questions to help the client evaluate the consultant's work, the success of the project, and the client's own satisfaction.

The bibliography on consulting at the end of the book suggests publications that are additional sources of information on consulting and related subjects.

1
What Is a Consultant?

The Consultant Defined

A consultant can be any person with special knowledge, skills, and talent who provides some particular expertise to people lacking and in need of it. A professional consultant, however, is an individual or a firm with special knowledge, skills, and talent who makes needed expertise available to a client for a fee, rendering advice and often helping to successfully implement that advice with and for the client.

What a Consultant Does

Richard V. Benson, a direct marketing consultant, describes his perception of a consultant's job in the chapter titled "What Does a Consultant Do?" in his book, *Secrets of Successful Direct Mail:*

> A truism: What a consultant does is most often shaped by the needs of the client.
>
> My basic perception of my role is to improve the efficiency of the client's direct marketing and to provide solutions to direct-mail problems. Beyond my direct marketing expertise, I am often involved in personnel, research and development, and business life cycles.
>
> In my case, I expect my clients to treat me as a vice president of their company. It is impossible to be even reasonably competent as a consultant if the client is not completely open about his business.

In addition to bringing new ideas to the client as well as a knowledge of what things are currently working or are test-worthy, the consultant frequently is a backup or nay-sayer to the client's instincts. Many times the consultant picks up a problem off the floor where it has been put aside for one reason or another and insists the client face up to it and make a decision.

It has always been my policy to give a client direct advice to the best of my ability without regard to whether it was what the client wanted to hear. My advice hasn't always been right, but it was always what I thought was best.

In my view, a consultant is a consultant, not a hands-on employee. In general my clients visit with me for a day or more three or four times a year. Generally speaking this is adequate since something needs to happen between visits so that there will be new information on which to base advice on next steps or new directions.

In between personal visits, there are telephone calls (very frequent with some) to handle any day-to-day questions. Many of my clients keep me updated by copying me with their internal reports. The clients for whom I do the best work are the clients who have done their homework and are well prepared when they see me.

As a general rule I am not involved in production—though if asked I will recommend suppliers. The same is true for copy. Many times I will give my personal briefing to a copywriter. I do not generate reports, but I am regularly involved in the analysis and interpretation of results.

In the past 15 years or more, I have rarely had a contract with a client, which meant if he didn't like my advice he could fire me the same day. I have been fired on short notice and some of those times are included in the following stories. The great benefit of this method of doing business is that it works both ways so that if I didn't think the client listened to me or if I didn't like the client's methods of doing business, I could resign without notice. In fact, I have resigned from as many clients, and with much less tenure on average, as I have had fire me. (I'm not sure that's cause for pride, but it has made me feel good.)*

---

* Reprinted with permission from Richard V. Benson, *Secrets of Successful Direct Mail* (NTC Business Books).

While far from representative of all consultants, Benson's view of his role as a consultant illustrates some typical characteristics of consultants: straightforwardness, candor, problem-solving abilities—particularly the ability to find the right questions as well as the right answers—and independence. We will see further characteristics and qualities of the consultant later in the chapter.

The Need and Demand For Consultants

The notion of making use of a consultant has grown greatly in the last twenty years. Consulting, which was an unusual occurrence twenty or thirty years ago, has become commonplace today, not only in large organizations but also in small organizations where the greatest growth has occurred. The increasing complexity and sophistication of our contemporary society—and the accompanying complexity of business and technology—often calls for the expertise and unique skills a consultant can provide. In business and technology, increased competition necessitates more knowledge and skills than many organizations can find or afford to hire full time; consultants can offer companies the talent and flexibility needed to succeed in a competitive field—a competitive world.

Consultants also offer valuable services to government and nonprofit organizations. These groups often cannot afford or do not need full-time employees with a whole range of unique and necessary skills, but consultants can and do deliver needed services for a shorter time and at lower cost than that of a full-time employee.

Consultants, however, sometimes are not the easiest people to work with. Often they are described as prima donnas who are difficult to get along with and who march to a different drummer. They are indeed a unique type of individual, and making the client-consultant relationship effective and efficient requires as much effort and attention on the part of the client as it does on the part of the consultant. But the effort to make the relationship productive is a worthy investment. Consultants can and do add meaningfully to the success of the projects with which they become involved.

Consultants' Services and Activities

Consultants provide a variety of skills and services to the client, among them:

Research:

    find suppliers
    find target markets for ideas or products
    find talent
    find experts
    find commercial possibilities for abstract ideas or concepts
    assess the public mood
    assess political realities
    trace problems, ideas, etc. to their source

Analyze:

    classify data
    perceive and define cause-and-effect relationships

Invent:

    design educational events
    improve on others' ideas
    update others' ideas
    adapt others' ideas
    create commercial possibilities for abstract ideas or concepts

Synthesize:

    summarize
    assess people's needs
    extract the essence from large quantities of data

Predict:

    plan financial matters
    predict obsolescence

Recommend:

> recommend experts
> recommend suppliers
> allocate scarce resources

Communicate:

> arbitrate disputes
> negotiate agreements
> terminate people/projects/processes
> translate jargon
> help others express their views
> help others clarify their goals and values
> handle difficult people
> interview

Motivate:

> sell an idea, program, or course of action to decision-makers
> raise money for nonprofit institutions
> raise money for business ventures
> recruit leadership
> direct creative talent

Evaluate:

> appraise monetary value
> judge people's effectiveness
> identify and assess others' potential
> analyze communication situations*

Qualities of the Consulting Practice

Consultants possess special expertise—knowledge, talent, skills—and make it in the form of services, available to clients. Consultants also possess other qualities that enhance the services they provide for their clients.

---

* Adapted from Richard N. Bolles, *What Color Is Your Parachute?* 2nd ref. ed. (Ten Speed Press, 1984).

Basic Qualities of the Consultant

1. Fact consciousness: An insistence upon getting the facts and checking their accuracy.

2. A sense of relevance: The capacity to recognize what is relevant to the issue at hand and to cut away irrelevant facts, opinions, and emotions that can cloud the issue.

3. Comprehensiveness: The capacity to see all sides of a problem, the many different factors that bear upon it, and the variety of possible ways of approaching it.

4. Foresight: The capacity to take the long view, to anticipate remote and collateral consequences, to look several moves ahead in the particular chess game that is being played.

5. Lingual sophistication: An ability to see beyond words and catch-phrases; a refusal to accept verbal solutions that merely conceal the problem.

6. Precision and persuasiveness: A mastery of the language, which includes the ability to state what one means, no more and no less, and the ability to convey one's ideas to other people and to convince them of the wisdom of those ideas.

7. Self-discipline: A commitment to thoroughness and an abhorrence of superficiality and approximation.

There are four other qualities that enhance the consultant's services and separate the consulting practice from other businesses.

First, consultants tend to work in rather small entrepreneurial environments. At one time they may have worked for large companies, but once they are in business for themselves, they have to provide for their own marketing and selling of services to be successful.

Second, consultants must enjoy—and excel at—problem solving and creative challenges. They are frequently asked to examine a complex situation, to define it, and to develop practical approaches or solutions. If a consultant cannot provide these skills or perform these activities, he or she is not going to have a successful consulting practice.

Third, consultants tend to be loners. They work in a vacuum. In most cases they do not have a large staff to implement their solutions or assess their strategies; they need to be self-reliant. Almost three-fourths of consulting practices consist of one or two professionals plus clerical support. Unlike people working for large organizations, they seldom have colleagues with whom to confer. Most consultants' interaction is with clients, and consultants need to have well-defined ideas and approaches to offer clients; they cannot toss around ideas with a client as they might with a colleague or peer.

Fourth, consultants are self-starters. They set their own schedules, decide their own goals, and create their own businesses. They provide services for their clients, but they are not typical employees.

Qualities of Success

A successful consultant serves the interests of the client. In consulting, no interest should come before that of the client, not even the consultant's self-interest.

The consultant pays attention to the client, listening to and really hearing the client's needs and desires and then responding to those needs, clarifying and redefining them if necessary. The consultant provides workable and effective solutions to the client's problem, fulfilling the client's needs and getting the job done in a timely fashion. The results of a successful consultation are a well-satisfied client and a well-compensated consultant.

Do You Need a Consultant?

If you think you need a consultant, you very well may. If you or your organization lack special skills or expertise, have specific needs and desires, or have a problem or difficulty that cannot be solved by internal staff capability, a consultant can probably be of service to you—provided you find the right consultant to meet your requirements. In the following chapters, you will discover some of the many reasons and ways in which clients make use of consultants, the different types of consultants, and information about the consulting process itself, to help you find the right consultant.

2
Why Do Clients
Use Consultants?

Differing Roles of the Consultant

I n my experience with hundreds of clients and thousands of consultants, I have discovered there are ten specific situations for which a consultant's services are likely to be needed. The reader should review each of these with his or her own needs and circumstances in mind to become aware of the many ways a consultant's services can be used.

The Need for Specialized Expertise, Talent, or Skill

The need for specialized expertise is probably the classic circumstance giving rise to the use of consultants. It occurs when a client discovers a need for certain types of skills that are not part of internal or staff capabilities at that particular time. The client faces the options of training staff for the task, bringing in full-time employees skilled for the task, or retaining a consultant—someone who already has the necessary ability and who will work with the organization using specific skills to accomplish the objective. Most often, the client decides to hire a consultant.

The decision to hire a consultant usually stems from the fact that the needed capability will be obtained more quickly and often at lesser cost than through internal training or hiring of full-time personnel. Another common reason is that the skill or talent is only required for a short period of time; since the need is short-lived, sporadic, or unpredictable, the time and cost of hiring or creating additional full-time personnel is unwarranted. Because the consultant is a specialist or authority in the particular problem area or technology, certain economies and efficiencies may be anticipated.

The Need for an Independent, Unbiased, Frank Opinion

The need for a frank evaluation, opinion, or judgment has been referred to in the literature of management as the all-important necessity of "going outside" to help clarify issues. Management finds strong motivation in the opinions and ideas of someone who is not beholden to the organization's political system, who is not biased by what has happened in the past, and who brings the different and refreshing perspectives of other industries and other organizations.

The Need for Temporary Technical Assistance

The need for temporary technical assistance—another common reason for the use of a consultant—is comparatively new, having become commonplace only within the last fifteen to twenty-five years. Temporary technical assistance became particularly prominent during the 1960s and the 1970s, and, given an expansionary economy, has been a major influence in the growth of the consulting profession during the 1980s and undoubtedly will continue to be a strong influence. In fact, the need for temporary technical assistance is now the most prevalent reason organizations hire consultants.

For a variety of technological and economic factors, complex organizations often find it necessary to respond quickly to opportunity and challenge. Yet quick responsiveness is impeded by the need to be both more cost conscious and efficient. Thus, organizations find themselves facing greater options and alternatives at a time when they are less ready to quickly respond. They find themselves having to build up their capacity for response very rapidly; they need to respond to an emergency situation or the necessity of completing work more quickly than would normally be their choice. When such circumstances occur, they need additional professional or managerial capability. This is particularly true in the high-technology sectors of the business world and in organizations involved in human services delivery.

A high level of government contracting and the ways in which government conducts its affairs and contracts has resulted in a substantial expansion of temporary technical consulting. Because budgetary appropriations are most often made late, and because much of what government wishes to accomplish takes longer than one fiscal year to complete, it becomes necessary for the government, when entering into contracts with private firms and local public agencies to accomplish its objectives (wind up its contracts) within eight, nine, or ten months. Even if the actual work is not fully accomplished in this amount of time, the funds must be spent. Even when government appropriations are timely, the actual work to be accomplished may consume fourteen or fifteen months.

Government—particularly the federal government—contracts with companies in the private sector, or local public agencies, and places them under severe pressure to complete their work very quickly. Most often these organizations are not staffed to handle this new business and additional responsibility, at least quickly, and they turn to consultants for additional staff and expertise. Such use of consultants is more prevalent in aerospace, information sciences, education, and health care.

After a few weeks or months, when the additional staff capability is no longer needed, the consultants are dismissed and the client's expense ceases. Temporary technical assistance is a convenient way for an organization to meet its temporary professional needs. It is not substantially different from the use of a temporary clerical agency.

Within certain industries, there are groups of these kinds of consultants, sometimes called professional gypsies, who move from industrial company to industrial company and from market to market on the basis of the economy of contract awards.

Economics can play a particularly relevant role in the decision to use temporary technical assistance. First, the need for the consultant's services is usually short-term (most often less than seven months). Second, the time and cost of identifying, recruiting, interviewing, testing, evaluating, orienting, and training the new professional/managerial employee is high. Add in the cost of supervision and related employment costs, and the use of consultants may seem to be a far more productive route to follow. Moreover, consultants, remember, are supposed to pay their own "marketing" or "acquisition costs" and should enter the client's world ready to work, fully trained, and in need of nominal orientation. Further, consultants normally need little or no supervision, but, of course, do need to be managed. The experienced client realizes that these behavior ideals are not always commonplace among consultants. but most would note that in comparison to full-time employees, consultants get to the task at hand more quickly and productively.

Business Cash Flow Problems

When an organization falters or has cash flow difficulties, it often retains the services of a consultant—sometimes called a turn-around consultant or a crisis-management consultant—whose sole or principal duty is to help the organization solve its business or cash flow problems.

While the problems are often more pervasive than the surface problem of cash flow, stubbornness, lack of appropriate predictive controls, or embarrassment about the problem may cause management to delay hiring a consultant. Indeed, the delay may be so great that management's options become limited, and it becomes other parties such as bankers or creditors who retain the turnaround consultant.

An important phenomenon of the time is the increasing regularity with which such cash flow or business problems are affecting the public sector of the economy. Fifteen to twenty years ago, such difficulties occurred almost exclusively in the private sector. There was a time when, if an agency ran out of money or ran into problems, it would simply go back to the voters to receive a transfusion of money, personnel, or policy. But voters have in recent years ceased wanting to be the bank of first resort, at least to the extent they were in the past. Therefore, for the first time, public agencies as well as private organizations are retaining the services of consultants when they encounter cash flow troubles.

It is becoming more commonplace, among both public agencies and private firms, for third parties to urge or insist that a consultant be retained. It is not at all uncommon for banks to select a consultant or suggest the use of a consultant for a troubled client organization that is a bank customer. Nor is it at all uncommon for a third party in a three-party contractual relationship to suggest or even to force the use of a consultant by another party.

I recall a consultation I conducted in which my client was a county office of education in California. This county office was in the third year of a three-year contract awarded by the state department of education for developing, testing, and implementing curriculum materials for handicapped students.

The first year was to be a research or need analysis effort, the second, a developmental effort, and the third a field testing effort of the actual curriculum materials developed in the second. The county office was about to start the third year, yet had hardly begun the developmental effort; at best estimate, it was only a third completed.

The state agency funding the project was agitated and concerned about the lack of progress. It informed the county office of education that if it expected to have its contract renewed for the third year, it had better hire a consultant who would be able to ensure timely completion of development and testing. The state specifically "suggested" that my firm be retained for this purpose. The county office of education had little choice. Abandonment of the contract was undesirable because of the embarrassment and loss of support funding.

This is one example in a long history of cases where a consultant is thrust upon a reluctant client. In this instance (though not always so), the working relationship was productive and harmonious; even though the client was not well disposed to the imposition of an outside consultant at the beginning, we worked very well together.

The Need for Expertise in Acquiring Resources

In a complex society such as ours, one observes many situations in which an organization must go to the marketplace to acquire resources of a specialized nature that it either has not needed to acquire in the past, or has not needed to acquire on a regular or repetitive basis. Such resources may be sophisticated or mundane and ordinary. The resource most frequently acquired (and likely the most ordinary) is capital. While money may seem to be a resource the organization acquires on a regular basis, and thus should be appropriately equipped to do so, such is simply not the case. Most organizations find capital acquisition to be a relatively rare and nonroutine event, so much so, in fact, that such organizations seek out consultant specialists to handle the task. Such consulting is so pervasive that it has become highly specialized. One finds a variety of different capital acquisition consultants operating in major markets, including accounts receivable consultants, financing/factoring consultants, SBA loan consultants, inventory financing consultants, capital equipment lease and finance consultants, syndication and private placement consultants—the list goes on. While capital acquisition is routine for some organizations, for others it is almost unheard of. For such organizations, the lack of experience, combined with the pressing importance of being successful in a very unpredictable arena, clearly necessitates outside expertise.

Clients use a wide variety of consultants to handle their myriad acquisition requirements. Another common one in the United States is for executive and managerial talent specialists—affectionately known as headhunters, more properly as executive search consultants. More rarely, acquisition consultants are asked to find natural resources, foreign sales representatives, underutilized plants, merger partners, and so on.

Because the need for such assistance is rarely permanent or even semiregular, the client often turns to a consultant. Normally, it would be impractical and expensive for the organization to hire full-time employees to be responsible for such ephemeral and transitory acquisitions or needs.

Handling Political/Organizational Problems

When people get into trouble in an organization, it is not uncommon for them to hire a consultant to save their own necks. Nor is it uncommon for someone else in the organization, even the immediate superior, to hire a consultant to assist a staff member who has encountered a politically sensitive situation.

Such troubles, of course, are seldom talked about publicly. You will never pick up the *Wall Street Journal* and find an advertisement that reads:

CONSULTANT NEEDED
Guess who's in trouble at the XYZ Company?
Consultants please apply at the side
door between 9 a.m. and noon February third.

Lower level management, for obvious reasons, often keeps such difficulties hidden from upper management. Sometimes such difficulties are hidden from peers in the organization as well, but from time to time it becomes necessary to bring in a consultant who can turn a situation around. The consultant may use technical skills or political skills.

Several years ago, I was retained by a client in the book publishing business who faced this very kind of problem. It was the western division office of a major New York publishing company. An assistant divisional manager responsible for a market research study had completely bungled the pet project of the New York–based vice-president for marketing, and, of course, New York was not pleased. However, the man's divisional manager in the western office was impressed with his work in other areas and decided to bail him out by bringing the market research project to a successful conclusion. Needing to produce quality results, they sought the services of an experienced consultant in the market research field.

I worked under the direction of the divisional manager and strictly behind the scenes. No one else knew of my involvement. Within two months, we were able to put together a finished research project and get it to the New York office. Not only was the project completed, but the assistant's career was saved.

Regulation

Largely born of the political environment of the 1960s, though with roots in the New Deal and beyond, regulation—governmental, trade and professional association regulation—is relatively new in consultant use. We are very busy passing laws in this country, laws that have as their principle objective control and regulation of the behavior of individuals, businesses, and labor organizations. These laws are quite inflationary, as we have discovered, and they create an enormous bureacratic overhead for our society; nonetheless, we continue to impose regulatory legislation. One of the primary uses of consultants today is to assist organizations to respond to new regulations. To give you a feel for the sheer amount of regulation, in one recent year, more than 434 new federal regulations were imposed on hospitals. The result? New reports to be written, new records to be kept, new inspections to be done—a tremendous work load, and an occurrence that has happened in virtually every sector of our society and our economy.

From time to time, we slip into an antiregulation philosophy, which means we may reduce the amount of regulation on hospitals this year from four hundred plus to perhaps one hundred. But such hiatuses are short-lived, and we continue to suffer from an increasing load of regulations from federal, state, and local government, as well as from all kinds of professional and trade associations.

An organization must run its day-to-day business, worry about finances, and respond to a thousand and one regulations. It cannot be expected to create a specialist to deal with each new problem that arises; thus, faced with a complex regulatory environment, the organization will frequently go outside for a consultant. A particular consultant may devote his total energies to some narrow field of regulatory authority. He or she stays current and aware and brings the perspective of a knowledgeable specialist to various clients. The experiences of one client tend to benefit the needs of another.

Tens of thousands of new consulting practices have been born of this regulatory phenomenon. For example, before the passage of federal environmental protection legislation, no one had really heard of environmental protection consultants. Perhaps a handful existed. However, in the three years following the passage of federal environmental protection legislation, more than seven thousand new consulting practices were born to deal exclusively with environmental protection legislation.

Eventually, of course, organizations that were making extensive and regular use of environmental protection consultants found full-time employees to handle their needs. In some cases, those consultants became full-time employees of the organizations. Universities opened departments in environmental science; they graduated people with degrees in environmental science who eventually went to work for corporations, governmental agencies, and the like on a full-time basis, which flattened out the growth market for environmental consultants. But evey time we pass legislation creating a new regulation to comply with, a demand for a new type of consultant is created because the penalties for not responding to regulations can be severe.

It has been estimated that more than 55 percent of billed time by the nation's lawyers and accountants is attributable to, and quite profitably so, the Internal Revenue Code. The rationale for hiring a consultat to handle the response to a particular regulation is akin to client's paying specialists to do their taxes.

Availability of Funds

For some reason, whenever we have a rapid buildup of money, there tends to be a desire to spend it very quickly. On occasion, this sudden-availability-of-funds syndrome prompts use of a consultant.

A rapid build-up of money can occur in a variety of ways. An organization may raise capital and get more than it really needs for its purpose; it may receive a large contract. Money in the pocket creates a vast array of ideas of how it can be spent, and since people tend to want to spend money very quickly, they are often predisposed to do some things that perhaps are not absolutely essential at the time, but which nonetheless are desirable to do. And people will frequently try to accomplish these things quickly by retaining consultants to assist them.

It is for this reason that consultants monitor the awarding of contracts, and it is for this same reason that consultants traditionally have fared wery well at the latter stages of a recessionary cycle in the economy. Historically, the government has fueled economic recoveries by awarding contracts to private businesses and local governmental agencies as a way of putting people to work. While such action does increase employment, it also generally increases the use of consultants.

Saving Key Personnel

The use of consultants for protecting or saving key personnel is quite close to an application mentioned earlier—political and/or organizational problems. The principle difference between solving political and organizational problems, however, and protecting and saving key personnel, is that political and organizational problems sometimes do not involve any direct threat to an individual—things simply may not be going well in an organization. But protecting or saving key personnel normally occurs because of a direct threat to someone's job or someone's status in an organization. It is not at all uncommon for an individual to bring in a consultant to help out his or her situation, to assist in some capacity, even to further his or her advancement within the organization.

Training

Most organizations are not equipped to train their personnel totally, so when they need training, they hire an outside trainer/consultant to design, develop, and conduct various training programs. Even organizations with large internal training departments find that certain types of training are not within their capability. Even if they can provide the training internally, they sometimes decide to go to external sources to introduce new talent and new ideas into the program or to meet training requirements that may tax their available resources.

As we have seen, there are many reasons for making use of a consultant. We may anticipate that new and more varied reasons for retaining consultants will likely unfold. Because consultant often represent a significant cost advantage to the client in comparison to full-time staff it is likely the trend to turn full-time staff into independent consultants will accelerate in the future.

The following example is indicative of this trend:

London-based Rank Xerox Ltd., the 50-percent–owned subsidiary of Xerox Corporation, started a program to encourage middle managers in such fields as planning, purchasing, personnel, and pensions to quit and become consultants. Limited to specializing in support functions whose presence on a day-to-day basis is not necessary, program participants are linked to headquarters via computer. Headquarters' costs are expected to decline by about 11 percent as a result of the change. The consultants, called Networkers by the company, stand to substantially increase their personal earnings. In most cases consultant fees for only two-days-a-week-service equal or exceed the former full-time salary. Rank Xerox pays for the computer. And these consultants have an additional three days a week to market and serve their outside clients.

The company saves by eliminating fringe benefit and reducing general overhead (telephone, physical space, etc.) and supervision.

Similar programs are being started or carefully considered by other firms here and abroad. I predict a strong trend in this direction, which can only benefit established consultants.

Summary

Here, then, are some situations that tend to require the use of consultants in organizations. I suggest you use this as a checklist to determine if you have any of the same needs or problems.

1. Do you need specialized expertise, talent, or skill?

2. Do you need an independent, unbiased, frank opinion?

3. Do you need temporary technical assistance?

4. Are you experiencing business cash flow problems?

5. Do you need expertise in acquiring resources?

6. Are you experiencing political and/or organizational problems?

7. Do you need to respond to regulation or do you have problems with regulation?

8. Do you have a sudden availability of funds and desire to use them with the help of a consultant?

9. Do you need to save key personnel?

10. Do you need help with training programs?

If you have identified one or more of the above situations then it may very well be time to bring in a consultant. This is not always necessarily true, but quite often it is the appropriate move to make. Or you may wish to bring in a consultant for purely economic reasons, because it is the most efficient thing to do.

By now, you may have identified a particular need for a consultant and the possibility of a real economic benefit; however, you must be careful. In my experience and the experience of firms I have worked with and researched, probably one third of the consulting business done in this country would not be undertaken if management took time to review its needs and circumstances and to think through its problems in a logical fashion. If done in a careful and timely manner the need for a consultant often would not be justified. In many cases managers simply delegate responsibility to a consultant just as they would delegate responsibility to someone on their staff. I once had an exit interview with a professional employee who reminded me during our exchange that the art of delegation entailed more than depositing the entire contents of my desk on his desk—the same is true in consulting.

If, however, after careful consideration, you believe you and your organization might benefit from the services of a consultant, the next step is finding the right consultant for your needs and desires.

3
Types of Consultants

There are several different kinds of consultants and there are very real differences among them, which you would be wise to take into consideration when selecting a professional practitioner. For example, the youngest professional consultant I have encountered, though there have been younger amateurs, was a man of eighteen. He was clearing a cool $60,000 a year (in 1978) as a skateboard park consultant. He counted among his clients several skateboard park owners and potential investors. His value to his clients came from his years as a youthful practitioner of the art of skateboarding and not from any formal education or on-the-job expertise. When seeking a consultant's services, you are going to encounter educated and experienced professionals, absolute amateurs, and everything between; you need to know what type of consultant you are looking for and the sorts of qualifications one will need to best serve your interests.

Operational vs. Advisory

The first distinction is between operational and advisory consultants. Most consultants today are operational, but twenty-five or thirty years ago almost all consultants were purely advisory.

An advisory consultant is an individual who comes into an organization, does whatever research or analysis is deemed appropriate, arrives at conclusions, makes recommendations, turns these recommendations over to the client, but never becomes personally involved in the day-to-day implementation of the recommendations. He or she simply delivers the grand plan and departs. In other words, the purely advisory consultant tells you what to do, but does not help you do it.

Operational consultants, however, not only conduct the research or analysis, arriving at conclusions and creating recommendations, but also, once they have turned these recommendations over to the client, stay with the client organization to assist the staff in properly implementing the recommendations. In some cases, operational consultants handle the entire implementation phase completely apart from the client's staff.

There are two primary reasons why most consultants today are operational. First, the recommendations often are not properly implemented in the client's organization without the consultant's assistance. Managers and organizations realize they are having difficulty fulfilling the recommendations and request that he or she stay longer to provide further help. Also, some consultants take upon themselves the responsibility of providing ongoing services because they have realized, through experience, that their excellent recommendations—at least what they consider to be excellent recommendations—are not being adequately carried out because the client's organization lacks the proper support, assistance, or direction to implement them.

Second, consultants have made themselves operational in the client's organization because it is financially rewarding to do so. The longer-term engagement produces more billable hours. Not only do they assist their clients, but they benefit themselves economically as well—enlightened self-interest, you might say.

If it is your intention that your consultant act merely in an advisory position, in most instances you will have to communicate such a desire. You will find that about one in ten of the consultants you encounter is purely advisory. If you expect an advisory consultant to handle the implementation stage of your assignment, you will be sorely disappointed.

Free-lancers versus Consultants

There used to be a big difference between a free-lancer and a consultant: consultants decided what would be done, and if the organization needed more staff or more expertise to accomplish the job, it would then hire free-lancers. Free-lancers did things, and consultants decided what should be done in the first place.

Now, however, the difference between a free-lancer and a consultant is very vague; there is a hazy distinction between the person who refers to himself or herself as a free-lancer, and the individual who refers to himself or herself as a consultant. Indeed, what you really need to do in such circumstances is find out whether this person is an operational or advisory consultant.

Part-time versus Full-time

It is estimated that as of the late 1980s there were approximately 400,000 consultants in the United States; some 280,000 (or 70 percent) of those are full-time. The balance, however, are part-time; they are people who work full-time for government, industry, educational agencies, and so on, who augment their incomes handling consulting assignments for others. Part-time consultants do consulting on the side, and are, in a sense moonlighting. About 60 percent of the time, part-time consultants moonlight with the permission and approval of the organization that employs them. They normally restrict themselves voluntarily or at the request of their employers in the kinds of consulting they do. Usually, they avoid consulting for direct competitors of their employers, customers of their employers, personnel who work for their employers, or suppliers to their employers. But beyond those restrictions, they often have a great deal of freedom.

One difficulty a client may have in working with a part-time consultant is that because of other obligations the part-time consultant is not always available on exactly the time frame or for the amount of time the client desires. However, to compensate, part-time consultants (whether consciously or accidentally) tend to charge less money for the services which they provide.

Full-time consultants, while generally charging more money, are also able to devote their undivided time (within reason) and energy to one client for the duration of a project. Assess your individual goals and needs—time, money, and extent of assistance desired and required—in determining whether a part-time or full-time consultant would most benefit you.

Process vs. Functional

Perhaps the most meaningful distinction is the difference between process and functional consultants.

Process consultants, sometimes called generalists, are skills-oriented. They go into any organization, any industry, any environment to deliver their skills. Skilled in one or several areas of technology, they take their expertise wherever it is needed. A good example might be that of a planner or statistician. The principles of statistics can be applied in almost any setting, and the technical knowledge of statistics is of greater importance to a statistician's work than are the characteristics of the setting in which the work is applied. To be truly useful, however, a process consultant must learn the language, the constraints, and the particulars important to the setting in which he or she applies his or her skills.

Functional consultants, sometimes called specialists, tend not to be as broad and expansive as process consultants. They often look at themselves not only as having skill, but as having skill in a particular, rather narrow, and unique environment. They will normally seek out only clients or consulting opportunities in organizations that are the same as or very similar to organizations with which they have been involved in the past. An example might be a hospital critical-care facilities planner. Unlike a process consultant, he or she will not use his or her particular skills to plan anything, anywhere; rather, this hospital critical-care facilities planner will make services available only to hospitals with critical care units.

In terms of your objectives as a user of consulting services, the difference between process and functional consultants really has to do with your own managerial style and approach. Do you believe in the benefit of "synergy from other disciplines and experiences?" Do you believe in technology transfer? If you do, you will probably find it more rewarding to retain the process consultant (generalist) who has had experience in a variety of fields, rather than a pure specialist who has only had experience directly related to your particular field, market, or industry.

What we can learn from board experiences is often of tremendous benefit and value; what we learn in one field of our endeavors applies elsewhere. I prefer to have a broad generalist who has had experience in many different fields because what that individual has learned in one industry, in one discipline—or really in several—can be applied to my problems, often with new ideas and refreshing insight.

But situations that require very specific expertise do exist, and there are certain clients who only want someone narrowly experienced in a particular area of endeavor. Question the consultant to find out what kinds of experience he or she has had and whether those provide the appropriate background or preparation to handle your particular needs.

Do not expect this difference between process and functional consultants to be easily apparent and clear. You will not find process consultants walking around with signs around their necks saying:

World's Greatest Generalist
Jack-of-all-Trades
I do Everything for Everyone

In reality, most process consultants do not consider themselves generalists. They regard themselves as multiple specialists, and this is probably a more accurate description. Therefore, once again, you should have a good idea of what you need and desire in a consultant as you search for a type of consultant whose skills and expertise satisfy you and your requirements.

Large Firm versus Small Firm

There are consultants from large firms, and there are consultants from small firms, sometimes called solo consultants—people working individually.

Large firms have much greater resources. They have back-up and support services, but they also have higher overhead and usually higher fees. Small firms and solo consultants tend to devote more of themselves and their talents to you; to them, you are not just another client. You are, perhaps, their principle client, or one of their principle clients, and they often take better care of you because of this. However, I know of large-firm consultants who will disagree with me on this point. They say they take care of all of their clients with equal care. But the evidence from some clients indicates otherwise. Clients do get more attention and better service from small firms. Yet in a small firm there is also the risk that you will not receive technical support as good as you might get from a large firm. Perhaps the smaller firm is very much like the country doctor or general practitioner who thinks he or she can do just about everything, when sometimes you really need a specialist.

Large firms tend to have a wide variety of specialists at their disposal, if not directly in their employ, so they can assist a client organization by bringing in the precise kind of talent for different situations. Again, it depends on the particular assignment or job that you have. Are you more in need of a multitude of specialist skills or someone who will give you greater attention, likely lower fees, and be more concerned about whatever it is you have to accomplish?

There is something to be said, too, about the size of your organization and the size of the consulting organization you select to serve you. Big kids like to play ball with other big kids; they are more comfortable that way. This is not to say that large client organizations do not make use of solo consultants. They do, and often. But it is far less likely that small client organizations will seek out the services of the consulting majors, although the majors are trying to overcome the inhibition.

Academic vs. Commercial

Most academically based consultants—by their very nature and existence—are part-time consultants. The academic environment is sufficiently unstructured so that the time availability of academically based consultants is quite good; for the most part, they can normally make themselves available whenever and wherever they are needed. Commercially based consultants, of course, can be either part-time or full-time, though most are in fact full-time. Some situations occur in which an academically based consultant may be most appropriate for you, such as when you need someone with strong academic skills, with a bent toward research, or with a solid background in theory. But there may also be situations in which the commercially based consultant will prove to be more appropriate for your needs because you need someone with hands-on experience, or a more practical approach. You should keep in mind that there are definite differences in the way academically based consultants approach their clients' problems and the way commercially based consultants do.

Of course, there are client organizations that use both kinds of consultants simultaneously. I have been involved in consultations and situations where there were three or four university professor-consultants working with the organization, doing almost purely theoretical or research work, along with several other commercially based consultants, working from a more practical point of view. Often, we were required to work with or integrate the two types of work. It can be a very productive and valuable mix.

Summary

You should now understand some of the basic types of consultants and their differences; you must determine which types are best suited to your needs. Here is a review of the different types of consultants and some questions to ask yourself in deciding what sort of a consultant might benefit you the most.

1. Operational vs. Advisory

   Advisory Consultants:
   - Do you just want or need advice, recommendations, and suggestions regarding your problem but want to act on the problem or implement recommendations yourself?

   If so, then you probably want an advisory consultant.

   Operational Consultants:
   - Do you want a consultant to assess your situation, make recommendations, and then implement those suggestions as well?

Then you most likely want to retain an operational consultant.

2. Part-time vs. Full-time

Part-time Consultants:

- Is your time schedule fairly flexible?
- Are you willing and able to accommodate a part-time consultant's other obligations?

If so, you may want to retain a part-time consultant, and your cost may be less in the bargain.

Full-time Consultants:

- Do you want, or does your project require, undivided time, energy, and attention?
- Are you able and willing to pay the possibly high price for undivided attention?

If so, then a full-time consultant may best suit you.

3. Process vs. Functional

Process Consultants (Generalists):

- Do you believe in technology transfer, in applying information or experience from one area to other areas?
- Would your project benefit from information gleaned from a variety of fields, industries, disciplines?

If your answers are yes, then you may do best with a process consultant.

Functional Consultants (Specialists):

- Do you require very specific expertise?

If you do, then you may require a functional consultant.

4. Large Firm vs. Small Firm

Large Firms:

- Do you require a wide variety of specialist skills?
- Will you require a large staff to implement recommendations?

If so, then you may need the help of a large firm.

Small Firms:

- Do you want or need very personal attention?
- Are lower fees more attractive to you?

Then a small firm may provide the personal attention and concern you want, and possibly at lower cost than a large firm.

5. Academic vs. Commercial

Academic Consultants:

- Do you require strong academic skills, a bent toward research, or a solid background in theory?

If so, and if you can accommodate possible part-time availability, then an academic consultant may suit your needs.

Commercial Consultants:

- Do you need someone with hands-on experience or a more practical approach?

If you do, then you may want to retain a commercial consultant.

4
The Consulting Process

The consulting process, depicted in the diagram in figure 4–1, is what happens between a consultant and a client. The process begins with the consultant. The consultant engages in some type of marketing and/or public relations activity to make you, the client, aware of the consultant's existence. If you do not call a consultant to request his or her services, be assured that one will call on you. Since consultants need to find clients to make money, they are continually marketing. Their marketing results in either your requesting the services of the consultant, or the consultant seeking you out and requesting to serve. Sometimes business comes to consultants by referral or response to their marketing; sometimes they have to go out and solicit it more directly.

Once there has been an agreement that the consultant can and may serve the client, or that the client is at least interested in the services of the consultant, there is usually an initial meeting in which face-to-face selling of the consultant's services takes place. If the parties are harmonious and if the client needs the services the consultant is prepared to deliver, the consultant may analyze the client's needs. This will most often result in a specific proposal on the part of the consultant, more often written than verbal, but it may be either.

If the client perceives the consultant's proposal as relevant but not sufficiently precise or direct, it will require some type of modification, negotiation, or redirection. Since the consultant leaves the initial meeting and conducts the needs analysis and proposal writing activity alone, in a vacuum, the proposal is likely

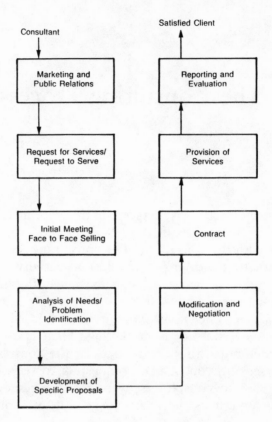

Figure 4–1. *The Consulting Process*

to require redirection. Errors in communication and changes in the client's perception of the project often result in the need for a revision of the proposal.

When the proposal modifications are satisfactory to both parties, the consultant and the client will enter into a contract or agreement. Such an agreement will usually be written, but many are verbal. After agreement is reached on terms and conditions, the consultant will render services appropriate to meet the objectives for which he or she was retained. In many cases, particularly for larger client organizations, there will be some type of formal reporting and evaluation. At the end, ideally, there should be a satisfied client and a compensated consultant. This is generally the process defining the consulting relationship. The consulting process is not—and never should be—a mysterious or unusual process; however, it is—and should be—a mutually beneficial business arrangement between consultant and client.

5
Finding Qualified Consultants

Recognizing the need for a consultant and understanding the basic consulting process are not necessarily difficult tasks; finding qualified consultants, however, is difficult. In this chapter and the next we shall deal with how one finds qualified consultants, and even more importantly, how one evaluates the findings in terms of suitability for individual needs and purposes.

Define Needs and Objectives

Finding consultants and evaluating prospects for their appropriateness is made far easier if the client has thought through his or her own problem or situation and has a firm grasp on his or her needs. Of all procurement decisions, the decision to retain a consultant is frequently the most difficult. All too often, clients are careless in their procurement practices. Perhaps they are careless whenever they buy anything, but they seem, to their consultants at least, to be particularly careless when they buy consulting. Too frequently clients commence their search with a very rough or vague idea as to what kind of help or assistance they will need or what it is they would like to accomplish. They will talk somewhat casually, perhaps to two or three different consultants, and then make a snap decision to bring someone in, though it often turns out that that individual may not necessarily be the right person for the job. Good analysis, good thinking, and good planning are the best ways to ensure that you are going to get a qualified consultant.

Consultants Come to You

Many consultants will simply solicit the business. Though it is rather a hit-and-miss proposition, they send letters and make phone calls. If they happen to contact you at the very time you need a consultant, then perhaps they will get some business from you.

To me, this circumstance is very similar to what I encounter with insurance salespeople. No one has ever sold me insurance, but a few people have taken my order. Just as you do, I get calls all the time from insurance salespeople. I always say, "I'm in the business," and that is the quickest way to end the conversation. But now and then, when I am sitting there actually thinking about purchasing insurance, an insurance salesperson will call and say, "I'm with Such and Such Life Company . . . " And I will say, "Fine, I'll take it." Then I can always sense that the phone is going to drop off the other end of the hook. The salesperson is an order taker.

That is what happens to some consultants. Consultants who are out there soliciting business tend to wind up being order takers. With certain probability, they will fall into someone's office at the very time someone needs their services and then will congratulate themselves on their sales abilities, when, in reality, they just happened to be in the right place at the right time.

Referrals

An excellent way for a buyer of consulting services to obtain a consultant is through referral. People you know—business associates, competitors, suppliers, other people who serve you (accountants, lawyers, bankers, and so on), customers, friends— may all use or have used consultants and may be in a position to refer a consultant to you. If they cannot give you a blanket referral, they may be able to give you the names of one or two people they understand do this kind of work, which will allow you to interview the consultants and make your own evaluation about their suitability. There are definite benefits to this manner of finding a consultant. You can seek out the recommendations of people you trust to give honest opinions. You can also seek out the recommendations of people who have faced problems similar to yours and who have solved them with the help of a consultant. There is a certain reassurance and some measure of accuracy when you start with a consultant recommended by people you know either personally or by reputation, who have worked with the consultant and found the services satisfactory, and/or when the consultant has some successful experience working with situations or difficulties similar to your own.

Of course, a referral is no guarantee the consultant will necessarily be the right one for you and your needs. Whenever possible, do seek out a referral, but bear in mind that personalities, needs, desires, and circumstances differ and that you must find a consultant who will satisfy your particulars. Also, when getting a referral, do not merely ask for a name; ask a few questions about the quality of the recommended consultant's services—how satisfactory were the consultant's performance and the project results? How easy was the consultant to work with? Would the person providing the referral hire this consultant again? A few questions will not tell you all there is to know about a particular consultant, but they will give you a better idea of whether the recommended consultant might be suitable for your needs, and whether you want to inquire further into his or her services.

Reading/Writing Ads

Many consultants find business from clients because the client has written and placed an advertisement to obtain a consultant with precise skills. This is a very direct way to get to the market. You can put an ad, let us say, in the business section of a daily paper, seeking a consultant with specific qualifications and expertise. To avoid wasted time talking to the unqualified and the unsuitable, you should make your advertisement as specific as possible. Screening must always be done, and the more your ad screens, the less you will have to do personally.

Sometimes consultants will advertise their services, and thus are contacted by clients who read their advertisements. Not very many actually advertise, but some do, and you may look in places such as the business section of the newspaper, professional and trade publications, and the like; you may find just the right person to serve your particular needs.

Directories

All professional associations within the consulting business publish a directory of their members, and most of them will make directories available to client organizations for free or at very low cost. By looking under professional and trade associations, national directories, or in the local phone book, you are likely to find some potentially suitable consultants whom you can then investigate further to find the one most appropriate for you.

The *Consultants and Consulting Organizations Directory* (Gale Research Co., Book Tower, Detroit, Mich., 48226, (313) 961-2242) is a national directory of consultants that is quite comprehensive because there is no charge to be listed. It contains a listing and description of more than fourteen thousand consultants and may be found in any good business library. It not only gives you the name, address, and telephone number of the consultant, but also includes a description of the consultant's services. You can look up consultants under a specific area of specialization, or you can find them geographically. Figure 5–1 shows a listing page from the Gale directory; such information about consultants is what you will find in it. If you were to buy the directory, you might find it rather expensive; however, you may read it for free at the library. There is no real reason to buy the book unless your need for a variety of consultants is so constant that you find it more efficient to purchase the directory than to run to the library.

Newsletter, yearbook, and periodical editors and directors and/or executives of trade and professional associations constantly come in contact with consultants or are knowledgeable of consultants in the field; some of these individuals are even consultants themselves. Thus, it can be helpful and valuable for you to get in touch with such people, and directories can aid you in finding them. A short bibliography of directories follows, and these volumes should be found in most larger libraries.

★13599★
HOWARD L. SHENSON
20750 Ventura Blvd., Suite 206   Phone:(818) 703-1415
Woodland Hills, CA 91364   Founded: 1971
Principal Executive(s): Howard L. Shenson. **Purpose and Activity:** Offers consulting to consultants and professional practices, those involved in the marketing of information products such as seminars and newsletters, and licensing of seminars, information products and educational/training materials. Practice specializes in effective marketing of intangibles including advertising, direct mail promotion and product/service introductions. Client base broad and varied: public corporations, government agencies, educational agencies, small business and individuals. Publishes newsletters and offers seminars and related publications. Also devoted to assisting clients to utilize innovative promotional techniques and delivery systems to communicate and deliver intangibles including such activities as developing and marketing: executive or organizational skills, educational programs, publications; training programs, financial programs and related product/service concepts. **Recent Publications:** H. Shenson, *How to Strategically Negotiate the Consulting Contract* (1986); *The Successful Consultant's Guide to Fee Setting,* Consultant's Library (1986); *Consulting: A Step by Step Guide to Building A Profitable Practice* (1986). Principal has authored numerous publications on various topics regarding consultancies. Many available on audio cassette tapes. **Conferences:** Licensing or Franchising; Marketing and Selling Through Seminars; Marketing Consulting Services; Creating Profitable and Successful Seminars; How to Select, Manage and Compensate Consultants and Trainers; Building a Profitable Professional Practice; Developing a Lucrative Paid Speaking Business; Beyond Consulting; Information Entrepreneurship. **Computer and Special Services:** Maintains consulting contracts on software; professional practice and consulting time and billing systems software; and performs competitive research on seminars and training programs being conducted.

★13600★
DAVID SHEPARD ASSOCIATES, INC.
2 Micole Ct.   Phone:(516) 271-5567
Dix Hills, NY 11746   Founded: 1976
Principal Executive(s): David Shepard, President; Fred Milman; John DiGiacomo; Geore Orme. **Staff:** 5. **Purpose and Activity:** Provides a full range of marketing consulting services including: strategic business analysis, new business/product development, data base design and implementation, financial planning/budgeting and analysis, marketing planning and testing, information and forecasting systems, financial modeling, list enchancement and segmentation analysis, fulfillment/customer service, circulation planning, market research, and performance audits.

★13601★
HENRY SHERRY ASSOCIATES, INCORPORATED
235 Peachtree St., N.E.   Phone:(404) 688-9885
Suite 1610   Founded: 1971
Atlanta, GA 30303
Principal Executive(s): Henry I. Sherry, President; K. Charles Kolkjen, Vice President. **Staff:** 6. **Purpose and Activity:** Firm is engaged in the practice of marketing consulting across a broad range of industries. Basic services offered are the development of annual and long-range marketing plans and strategies; solving particularly perplexing marketing problems in areas such as product life cycles, market segmentation, distribution, sales personnel and organization, pricing, etc.; development of industry studies aimed at new product entry, divestiture or acquisition; market research studies of all types; preparation and implementation of sales training programs; and participating directly with clients in the implementation of marketing plans and programs.

★13602★
PETER SHERWOOD ASSOCIATES, INC.
20 Haarlem Ave.   Phone:(914) 761-3033
White Plains, NY 10603
Principal Executive(s): Peter W. Sherwood, President. **Purpose and Activity:** Chemical and economic marketing consultants. Areas of specialization include petrochemicals, organic intermediates, and polymers. Active in market studies, market analyses, diversification studies, locating new products and technology, economic evaluations,

profitability and feasibility studies, business information programs, and process studies.

★13603★
SHIRLEY ADVERTISING AND PUBLIC RELATIONS
Box 515298   Phone:(214) 386-0878
Park Central   Founded: 1977
Dallas, TX 75251
Principal Executive(s): Shirley Lande, President; Keo Lande, Treasurer. **Staff:** 3. **Purpose and Activity:** A full-service advertising, consulting and public relations firm, large enough to provide outstanding quality but small enough to give each client first-team attention and service. It tailors the message to the product—exploring creative possibilities within a carefully analyzed marketing framework. Serves all areas of advertising, writing and producing television and radio commercials, audio-visual presentations, brochures, annual reports, and print ads for magazines and newspapers. Public relations areas include such activities as press kits, publicity, press releases and strategy. All work has a strong marketing and research base, especially in media selection.

★13604★
SHOPPING CENTER CONSULTANTS
5911 Oakland Park Dr.   Phone:(703) 250-5166
Burke, VA 22015   Founded: 1977
Principal Executive(s): Carleton (Bob) Meyers, President; Helen Demory, Vice President. **Staff:** 7. **Purpose and Activity:** Provides marketing consultation for shopping centers to accelerate leasing, maximize customer traffic and sales through effective marketing techniques. Comprehensive services include leasing systems and packages; grand opening sales promotions programs for merchants; image enhancement publicity; and feasibility studies. **Recent Publications:** C. Robert Meyers regularly publishes articles in *National Real Estate Investor, Retail Leasing Reporter, Shopping Center World,* and *Value Retail News.* **Conferences:** 30 Marketing Ideas in 60 Minutes.

★13605★
RICHARD L. SHORTEN
170 Pulis Ave.   Phone:(201) 444-2101
Franklin Lakes, NJ 07417   Founded: 1970
Branch Office(s): Chicago, Illinois; Dallas, Texas; Fort Lauderdale, Florida; Los Angeles, California; New York, New York; Pittsburgh, Pennsylvania. **Principal Executive(s):** Richard L. Shorten. **Staff:** 39. **Purpose and Activity:** A consulting firm that prefers to work on particularly difficult problems and complex marketing situations.

★13606★
RICHARD SIEDLECKI, DIRECT MARKETING
2674 E. Main St.   Phone:(805) 658-7000
Suite C-170   Founded: 1977
Ventura, CA 93003
Principal Executive(s): Richard Siedlecki. **Staff:** 4. **Purpose and Activity:** Direct marketing consultants offering services in sales lead development programs, direct mail marketing and advertising, mail order, and new product launches for financial, industrial, consumer, and business-to-business firms. Range of activities includes both direct consumer and business-to-business. **Recent Publications:** *The Lead Letter Newsletter* (monthly publication on direct mail, mail order, telemarketing, selling, and catalog marketing, as well as special reports on direct response marketing). **Conferences:** Offers seminars and lecture programs on direct marketing at various California area colleges and to business executive groups.

★13607★
GARY SIEGEL ORGANIZATION, INC.
6025 N. Christiana   Phone:(312) 539-2922
Chicago, IL 60659   Founded: 1983
Principal Executive(s): Gary Siegel, President; Laura Appelbaum, Vice President. **Staff:** 7. **Purpose and Activity:** Performs custom opinion research, specializing in the precise measurement of attitudes and opinions and generating the optimal communications strategies for persuasive campaigns to change attitudes and behaviors. Serves professional firms, professional associations, political and public;

Figure 5–1.

Standard Directories

The Encyclopedia of Associations
Gale Research Co.
Book Tower
Detroit, Mich. 48226
(313) 961-2242

National Trade and Professional Associations of the U.S.
Columbia Books, Inc.
1350 New York Avenue, N.W., Suite 207
Washington, D.C. 20005
(202) 737-3777

The Newsletter/Yearbook Directory
Newsletter Clearing House
44 West Market Street
Box 311
Rhinebeck, N.Y. 12572
(914) 976-2081

The Standard Periodical Directory
Oxbridge Communications, Inc.
150 Fifth Avenue
New York, N.Y. 10011
(212) 741-0231

The Directory of Management Consultants
Kennedy Publications
Templeton Road
Fitzwilliam, N.H. 03447
(603) 585-2200, 585-6544

Research for the Ideal Consultant

In a more personal approach, you can also conduct research to find the ideal consultant—another way many good consultants are found. Sit down and determine what you need to have done and who, in your wildest dreams, would be in a position to accomplish what needs to be done. Then you may indeed discover that there are some people you would not otherwise think of or find in a directory or advertisement or through a referral—perhaps a university professor or the head of some other business organization or government agency—who might be interested in handling your assignment, if only on a part-time basis. If you really sit down and think about the job, using your investigative thinking skills to figure out who might be in a position to help you, you may well come across the ideal kind of consultant for a particular project.

Leading Authorities

There are leading authorities in particular fields that you might want to contact, either to serve as your consultant or to recommend a consultant. Leading authorities are those people who write articles in trade and professional journals and give speeches and lectures before trade, professional, business, civic, and community groups. Leading authorities are also people who are guests on radio and television talk shows, are interviewed in the newspaper, and so forth. They often have the expertise you are looking for and may be willing to provide you with it.

Trade and Professional Associations

If you are looking for someone with particular kinds of skills, you might try talking to the heads of the trade and professional associations, since they have access to the many consultants within their associations. *Encyclopedia of Associations* and *National Trade and Professional Associations of the U.S.* can help you to find such people. Moreover, many of these associations provide a referral service for their members, and by looking into these services, you may find a consultant suited to your needs. In addition, most professional associations have ethical standards and requirements for maintaining membership in the association; a consultant's membership in a trade or professional association is no absolute indicator of his or her competence or quality of service, but it can help give you a start.

Brokers

Brokers create a coterie of consultants with various kinds of skills, and then represent these consultants to business and government agencies in need of their services. Brokers are frequently found in the technical fields of consulting, as well as in specialized areas such as consulting services to attorneys. When an attorney needs a consultant, he or she might well go to a specialized broker who has a group of expert witnesses and authorities on matters that commonly occur in litigation. Normally the broker collects a percentage of the fee. So if you are paying the consultant $500, it is not at all unlikely that the broker is going to take $150 of that back from the consultant for getting the consultant the job in the first place.

Summary

There are nine primary ways to find a consultant:

1. Define your needs and objectives—determine what you want in a consultant.

2. Wait for consultants to contact you.

3. Seek out referrals.

4. Read ads for consulting services or write your own ad to obtain a consultant with specific skills.

5. Use directories to look for consultants.

6. Determine your ideal consultant and seek out that person.

7. Seek out leading authorities either to serve as your consultant or to recommend a consultant.

8. Look for a consultant via trade and professional associations.

9. Find a consultant broker.

6
Evaluating Potential Consultants

The degree of precision with which you evaluate the suitability and capability of the potential consultant is likely to be
an important, even determining, factor in your ultimate satsifac-
tion with the results achieved from the consultation. Over the
years, I have heard numerous complaints from clients regarding
the quality of services provided by consultants. In most cases
such dissatisfaction can be directly related to factors that could
have been determined in the course of careful preconsultation
evaluations and interviews.

The reader might well ask, then, why, if danger signs were
apparent and even obvious in the first place, were they not discovered? There are, undoubtedly, many reasons, but the most
significant is the imprecision or sheer laziness with which the
client approaches the task of evaluating his or her own needs and
the suitability of a potential consultant. If the client fails to fully
understand the precise outcomes the consultant must produce,
the result may be dissatisfaction and a counterproductive expenditure of funds. It also provides clear evidence that the client does
not fully understand his or her own problem or comprehend the
full range of needs to which a response was desired.

In reality, many consultations could be avoided (or reduced
in scope), saving considerable dollars, if clients were disciplined
enough to think their needs and problems through with sufficient
precision to identify the ways in which a consultant's services are
really needed. Further, such precise analysis will often serve to
identify a more specific or narrow set of skills required from a
consultant. This can be advantageous in that the assessment of

a narrower set of skills may result in the client's ability to obtain a professional at lower cost or to avoid the expense of planning and elaborate needs analysis expenditures often associated with consulting. One consultant with whom I am familiar often says, "I wish my large corporate clients were more like my smaller entrepreneurial clients." This is a very telling statement. Like many consultants, this one finds that working with a precise, no-nonsense, frugal client is often more productive than working with casual, often undisciplined, free-spending bureaucrats. In short, more corporate clients would be well-served behaving as if the money they spent were their own, not someone else's.

Successful use of consultants often requires as much work on the part of the client as it does on the part of the consultant, at least in terms of planning and strategy. Consultant and client must understand the need, the objectives, the limitations, and the nature of the results to be achieved. This can only occur when both parties have a shared understanding of all the parameters related to the consultation. The more the client is able to provide precise, even measurable, objectives to the consultant, the greater the likelihood that the consultation will produce the desired outcomes in a cost-efficient fashion. And contrary to conventional wisdom, though certainly exceptions do exist, most good consultants do not seek to build continuing client dependency on their services. Like good clients, good consultants are busy, over-committed, and not in need of more ways to spend their time. With proper evaluation on the part of the client, limited experience with a consultant can be productive and rewarding.

The Evaluation Process

How, then, do you evaluate a potential consultant? How do you find out whether someone is the right consultant for you? There are many ways. I think that the best way is to use what I call a "here and now" basis of evaluation—meet your potential consultant in person.

You must schedule an interview with the prospective consultant. When you call to make an appointment, briefly describe your problem or reason for seeking consulting services and make clear that you are seriously seeking a suitable consultant for your needs and would like to set up a personal interview. In a sense, evaluating a potential consultant is no different from evaluating a prospective employee. You need to sit down face-to-face, ask the hard questions, listen for the right answers, and reject those people who do not provide them. I wish I could tell you there is an easier way of evaluating consultants, but there simply is not.

The operating style of consultants is an important factor in evaluation, too. In addition to their technical know-how, ideas, concepts, and approach to the problem, consider how they operate. There are consultants who are too creative, too entrepreneurial, too shoot-from-the-hip to be comfortable with a stodgy bureaucratic organization. There also are consultants who are too bureaucratic themselves, too conservative to suit a creative, innovative organization. A mesh between the personality or management style of the consultant and the personality and management style of the client is essential. If they lack compatibility of style and approach, they are likely to have difficulty working together to produce the necessary results.

The First Meeting between You and the Consultant

The first face-to-face meeting between client and consultant can be a productive, rewarding, and instructive session. To be effective, however, the client must come to the meeting with full understanding that this is a meeting between equals and peers and not a meeting between superior and subordinate. Also, the client must be aware that the consultant's time is of equal value to the client's and that the consultant (read "a worthwhile consultant") has as much right to reject the client's business as the client has to reject the consultant's services.

With this environment of mutual respect, the first meeting allows the parties to get to know one another and to determine whether they will find it of mutual benefit to work together. While it is obvious that you will interview the consultant, a good consultant will also interview you. You should be a little suspicious if he or she does not. Any consultant who does not find out what you want, what you have already done relative to your needs and problems, and what business arrangements are to your liking is probably too hungry and too willing to be a good consultant.

The First Four or Five Minutes

The first four or five minutes of the first meeting between the client and consultant may be crucial, but be cautious. You may well reject a qualified person within the first four or five minutes simply because he or she does not give a good interview. That will be your loss because someone who might have been very qualified leaves without ample consideration on your part. Clients need to remember that many consultants are not as adept at salesmanship, even subtle salesmanship, as others. In general, consultants prefer doing their work to marketing their skills. In a day and age when the client encounters very polished presentation tactics, it is important to look beneath the surface for substance.

It is unlikely however, that you are going to make the mistake on the other side of the coin. That is, if you invite a consultant to meet and talk to you, and he or she sounds suave and sophisticated, organized, and confident in the first few minutes, you will keep the consultant talking. You will perhaps talk to him or her two or three more times, but if you are at all good at interviewing and observing people, you will figure out that this person is not qualified or not the right person for your job. You will have wasted your time, but you probably will not have made a mistake.

So, while the first four or five minutes are crucial, I think they tend to be so only in the sense of possibly causing you to dismiss someone who is very qualified because you do not allow him or her adequate time to demonstrate skills and competency.

Evaluating a Consultant's Skills

Next, you will find questions that could be asked of consultants during the initial interview—questions, that, I have found very quickly help to discover if the consultant is qualified. You will undoubtedly want to modify these questions to some extent, but nonetheless, the answers you will get will be useful. And you will discover that retaining a consultant is not very different from retaining an employee in terms of the questions you ask and the criteria you assess. You must always rely on your ability to evaluate people and decide whether they are honest, come up with ideas that make sense, and make proposals relevant to your problem and needs.

Seven Quick-Check Questions to Evaluate a Consultant's Skills

1. What do you regard as our principal need or problem?

2. What can you offer us that other consultants we have interviewed/your competitors have not been able to provide?

3. How will we measure or evaluate your success in meeting our needs/solving our problems?

4. Are you willing to work on a performance basis—that is, to be compensated on the basis of the results you produce?

5. What related experience have you had in working with organizations similar to ours or with other organizations in this industry or field?

6. What related experience have you had in working with needs and problems similar to ours?

7. Who may we contact as a reference about the services you provide?

Additional Questions to ask Yourself and/or the Consultant

- How can I profit?
- Why can I profit?
- Where can I profit?

- Who says I will profit?
- What will I profit?
- When can I profit?
- Do I need this service?
- Do I really want this service?
- Can I really afford this service?
- Will I make use of the outcomes?
- Am I being given a good deal?
- Should I check out the competition?
- Could I get this service for less?
- Is this consultant honest, reliable, and right for me?
- Is the consultant knowledgeable?
- When do I need to make my decision?

Outcomes and Expectations

Most certainly in this first meeting there will be a discussion of the outcomes and expectations of the consultation. What is this consultant expected to produce? You are going to get a better performance and better results if you can tell the consultant, as specifically as possible, what a consultant must accomplish or produce to satisfy you.

If you do not tell the consultant this, he or she should ask. One of the signs of a weak consultant, in my mind, is when the consultant fails to ask what the client wants to accomplish, if the client has failed to communicate these goals precisely. If all the consultant wants to do is sign the contract, get under way, and figure out later what has to be done, you are likely to encounter problems.

However, often a client decides on the nature of his or her problem or need before ever calling a consultant; once this decision is made, a client may tend to become committed to it. Then, if the consultant discovers that the problem is different from the client's perception of the problem (and such is frequently the case), there can be some conflict in the relationship as the consultant attempts to change the client's thinking or behavior about the particular problem. This ego conflict may also work the other way. Once the consultant has done a formal needs analysis—a diagnostic—for the client, the consultant may become very committed to it. Consultants should be able to bury their egos for the benefit of the assignment or the client, but they are human (though some people would dispute this) like everyone else. So the relationship may become strained if the client disagrees with the consultant's needs analysis. The first meeting will be greatly enhanced if both client and consultant are not overly committed to their previous thinking. Moreover, a good consultant should do the needs analysis in what I would call a "real time" fashion—as needs are discovered, as the situation is understood, a good consultant should confirm these with the client so that the final report of the needs analysis does not come as an absolute surprise to the client.

Measurable Objectives

Whenever possible, the client and the consultant should work together to establish tangible, measurable, observable criteria—things like dollar profit, sales quotas, number of units produced, and number of people who pass the test at the conclusion of a training program as a result of the consultation—to serve as the basis of evaluation. However, frequently there are no tangible factors appropriate for evaluation, in which case, the second best thing to do is to arrive at some proxy measurement.

For example, if we are going to bring in a consultant to train teachers so they will be able to give their students better vocational job placement and better work experience later on, how will we know when we have been successful? We may have to wait five to seven years to find out if, in fact, the students do get better vocational placement. Obviously, we cannot wait five to seven years to determine whether the consultant should be paid; payment has to come out of this year's budget. So we may develop some kind of a proxy measurement. We may just find a test instrument and if the teachers can pass the test, then we will believe they have the right attitudes, the right skills, and the right knowledge to be able to bring about improved performance on the part of the students.

That is a proxy measure. When a proxy measure is inappropriate, we can, of course, resort to our old standby—gut feelings and instinct. "I am happy. I am satisfied." What you and the consultant should discuss very precisely before the consultation is what you, the client, will have to see to assure you and satisfy you that the consultant has done the job well. Now perhaps that is something very specific: "We must have a 14 percent increase in profits or you fail," or maybe it is, "I just have to feel better." Although it is difficult to say in the abstract, strive to make your goals as tangible and specific as possible; if that is not possible, find a proxy if you can.

Business Arrangements

It is important for both parties to discuss the nature of the financial arrangements and the contractual terms and conditions. Consultants collect their fee in a variety of ways—by the day, by the hour, fixed-price, and so on. Each method of payment results in the client taking more or less risk. A solid understanding of each party's risk-taking propensities and the ways they might work together should be an integral part of the first meeting.

Experience and References

Once you are satisfied that the consultant's here-and-now answers to your questions are appropriate, that the consultant's operating style is suited to your organization and your particular needs—indeed, that this may be right consultant for you—you will certainly want to inquire into his or her experience and may well want to check some references. You may also ask for and check the consultant's references before the first meeting. Perhaps after checking references, you will already know this consultant is not right for you, in which case you need never have a face-to-face meeting. However, it is probably no wiser to dismiss a potential consultant whom you have never met on the basis of references alone (except in the very rare case that all the references are negative) than it is to retain a consultant after a first meeting without ever checking his or her references. It is at your discretion whether you ask for references before the interview or during the interview, but do check into them. You will find the results well worth your time and effort.

There are different kinds of references consultants can give you. There are supplied references, which are what I have when I reach into my briefcase and take out a typed sheet of names, addresses, and telephone numbers in response to a client's request for references. I say, "Here they are. Please feel free to contact any of these people." This is the least useful form of reference to a client because obviously the consultant is not going to list anyone who would say anything negative or critical. This does provide a way of checking out the consultant, but not a great way unless you happen to know personally and professionally one or more of the people on the reference list, and you think you will get a totally straight answer and honest opinion.

Another form of reference is what I would call a peer reference: talk to other consultants who may know the consultant whom you are considering. This is not at all an uncommon practice. Consultants tend to know one another to some extent, or to have heard of one another, or at least to know third parties who know both of them. And consultants are fairly good judges of other consultants; moreover, unlike doctors, they are not nearly as closemouthed about the problems and the limitations of their peers. So you may well find it within your interest to talk to other consultants.

Perhaps the best source of reference is former clients of the consultant. If the consultant is willing to tell you who the former clients are, or if you know who the former clients are, this is an excellent place to check references. Many consultants, however, and properly so, do not reveal the names of clients. They regard their clients and the work they have undertaken for them as confidential. You should pay careful attention to what a prospective consultant says about past clients. If the consultant lacks discretion and becomes your consultant, he or she may be indiscreet regarding you and your organization.

There are three other evaluation procedures that may be quite useful. The first is to research the consultant. Examine what he or she has done, for whom, and where. Talk to people who know the consultant; that is, create your own list of references.

Second, evaluate the consultant's contributions to his or her field. What has the consultant written and/or researched? Where does he or she speak? With whom in the field does the consultant keep company? Heads of trade and professional associations and scholars in the field may be helpful resources. Third, take a good look at who is running the consultant's practice. How much in control of his or her destiny is the consultant? A consultant who is too complacent is likely to be unsuccessful and not very busy. When I retain a consultant, I want someone who is in control, intelligent, innovative, assertive, and who knows what he or she wants and at which points he or she plans to make a stand.

Client Fears

In a survey of 610 clients, I discovered that there are specific fears clients have about using consultants. These are presented next in priority order. The first meeting is an excellent place for you to ask questions to determine whether you have these fears about a particular consultant.

Consultant Incompetence

The most prevalent fear is that the consultant is incompetent; he or she looks and sounds good, but really is useless. Have the consultant give you sufficient information about his or her knowledge, skills, and experience for you to rule out the fear of consultant incompetence.

Continuing Dependency

Clients fear they will get hooked on consulting and will continuously need help, never being free of the consultant. You need to press the consultant for ways in which the consultant will make this a turnkey activity. Find out how he or she will turn things over to you and train and inform you and your staff so that you are not continuously dependent on the consultant's services.

Lack of Managerial Control

Clients also fear the consultant will be so powerful and so overwhelming and so much in control that the client organization will lose control of the situation. Management is not and should not be the consultant's role. It is not the consultant's responsibility to make decisions; that is management's responsibility. The consultant's role is to advise management about decisions to be made and to provide documentation, evidence, support, and recommendations, without taking away decision-making authority from the client. So make sure you and your consultant understand these essential distinctions.

Excessive Fee

If you fear the consultant's fee is too high, have him or her justify for you exactly what will be done. The consultant should be willing to break down the cost and show why the services cost what they do, until you are comfortable with the cost analysis. You may discover that the fee seemed excessive because you have said certain things about the project to the consultant or the consultant has made certain assumptions about the project that are not in fact accurate.

You may also find that you and the consultant have different expectations about the quality of the result to be produced. Consultants, whenever possible, like to deliver Rolls Royces to their clients. But some clients prefer Pintos. If that fact is not communicated, the consultant will seemingly be charging too much money for the services the client is expecting, and the client will be unhappy.

If the client is the Department of Defense, and it is trying to figure out where to put antimissile missiles, then I would expect it to want to have about 99.9 percent accuracy in its decision. It is going to pay a great deal of money to get 99.9 percent accuracy. Getting 90 percent certainty about a decision carries a substantially lower cost than buying that extra 9.9 percent, which has a proportionately much greater cost. If, however, the client is the City Parks and Recreation Department, and it is trying to figure out how many people used the park this summer, then perhaps it is willing to live with 80 percent certainty and considerably less cost; it is not as vital that it buy 99.9 percent accuracy.

You must make clear to your consultant what level of response, what level of result you are looking for. If you do not communicate this information, the consultant should determine this information from you, but sometimes consultants make assumptions. Do not allow this to happen. To alleviate excessive fees, specify to the consultant what level of quality and expense you deem desirable and necessary, and find out from the consultant what agreement or what discrepancy exists between your needs and the consultant's needs.

Time Availability

Many clients fear the consultant will have insufficient time to complete the client's project on time. Therefore, have your consultant justify how much time the consultation will take, when the project will take place, where the major milestones will be, and when the project can be expected to be completed. Agree to what will happen, if anything, if it is necessary to adjust the time schedule.

Evidence of Failure

Sometimes clients are afraid that the need for a consultant will suggest to others in the industry, or in the client's organization, that such a need is a failure on the part of the client. This is rarely accurate or true. It should be the good consultant's job to ensure that the client will be protected from any embarrassment, that the consultant will work behind the scenes in a manner supportive to the client's self-interest, and, further, that the consultant will place his or her ego backstage to make the client look good.

Disclosure of Proprietary/Sensitive Data

Some clients fear that in using consultants they may be disclosing sensitive or proprietary data that could, in the wrong hands, damage their interests in some way. For this reason, a consultant's discretion is very important. Any sign of indiscretion is perhaps a sign that you cannot release sensitive material to the consultant. You may even wish to have your consultant sign a disclosure statement that says the consultant will not release confidential data. Although the disclosure statement itself will not prevent the consultant from being indiscreet, it will make this concern more prominent.

Improper Diagnosis/Needs Analysis

Low on the list of fears is the concern that either the client or the consultant may have improperly diagnosed the need for the consulting services, resulting in wasted time, effort, and money. Thus, it is important that both parties confirm the needs analysis/diagnosis, regardless of which party originally undertook the analysis. Whenever possible, needs analysis and problem definition should be done by client and consultant, working together.

Lack of Impartiality

And finally, the last of clients' fears about making use of consultants is that the consultant will lack impartiality. The consultant has, as a requirement and responsibility of being a professional consultant, an obligation to serve only the client's best interests. The consultant should not be beholden to any other interests whatsoever or have any side deals, commissions, kickbacks, referrals, or the like, which could cause the consultant to lose objectivity—the true value to the client.

Therefore, examine your consultants. Scrutinize them to make sure they are not tied in or influenced in any way that might cause them to make decisions other than in your best interests.

Client Fears Alleviated

While you may not completely eliminate your fears about retaining a consultant (and a certain measure of caution is not unwise), by evaluating your potential consultant, communicating your needs and concerns, and questioning and listening to the consultant's answers, you should be able to alleviate most of your fears. Of course, if after carefully evaluating the prospective consultant you still have considerable wariness about hiring him or her, then it is probably time to move on to another.

Consultant Fears

The most common consultant fears are that the client will cheat the consultant and not pay, that the consultant will get bogged down in the client's organization because of an inability to define the problem and agree to the scope of work. Consultants also fear the client won't provide adequate support to the consultant, or that the people with whom the consultant has to work in the organization will be counterproductive to what the consultant is trying to achieve. As a client, it is your responsibility to make sure that your consultant need have none of these fears. Even if the consultant does not communicate any fears to you (and chances are, the consultant will not), you should be prepared to define objectives, to provide support and a supportive staff, and to pay fully for satisfactory services rendered.

The Consultant's Marketing

The consultant expects it will take, on the average, about a day of his or her marketing time to sell five days of time. Thus, if your consulting project involves fifty days of the consultant's time, it may well be that in the process of proposal writing, interviews, phone calls, the consultant could spend up to ten days' time in the marketing stage. That is a considerable amount of meetings and a considerable amount of getting to know one another. In ten days' time you get to know someone fairly well, so if in ten days you have not figured out whether this person is competent, you are probably never going to figure it out, not even after the consulting work is done.

The longer the consultation, the smaller the percentage of time usually required in marketing. The reverse is also true: many consultants will tell you that it is just as difficult to sell a twenty-five–day assignment as it is to sell a ten-day assignment. One of the factors that adds to the consultant's marketing time, of course, is a client's lack of precision and direction. A proposal I completed while writing this chapter illustrates the point. A Fortune 100 company flew five of its executives to Los Angeles for a meeting with me at an airline club at Los Angeles International Airport. Despite my constant efforts to pin them down about objectives and desires, it became apparent to me that they had no inclination to be specific. Either they had not thought through their objectives and needs with sufficient precision to be specific, or they were testing my ability to be expansive and creative. We left the meeting with my commitment to send them a proposal to outline "how my services would be of value."

I know of no more difficult proposal to write. The information was too vague. For two weeks I did no writing but thought (mostly subconsciously) about what my proposal would say. In one day, it flowed out. I proposed twelve "mini-projects" that would serve their needs. The response took less than a week (rather spectacular turnaround for a large company), and the outcome was favorable: four of the specific projects were agreed to with certainty, with four others highly likely in the second year. As many consultants have learned, they often have to stimulate the client's thinking with a potpourri of interesting ideas to focus the client more specifically on desires, needs, and objectives.

Should you expect to pay for the consultant's time during the marketing phase? You will, whether you expect to or not. You will pay for it indirectly in the form of overhead after the contract is awarded, or you will pay directly. Only a small percentage of consultants, however, charge directly for their marketing time. If it is not a direct charge, the consultant will treat marketing as an overhead expense and will charge all future clients indirectly. So yes, the clients will pay for it. Someone has to pay for marketing.

It is not at all uncommon for one federal agency I know of to cause an expenditure of $150,000 worth of consulting time in proposals and marketing to award a $30,000 contract. The agency contractors go to fifty people asking for proposals. Each spend approximately $3,000 to respond to the government's

R.F.P. That makes $150,000 that has been spent to get a $30,000 contract that is awarded to one person. This is one of the reasons consultant's fees tend to be somewhat high. Shopping is much more common in the public sector than in the private sector, where few clients shop. A statistic that amazes me is that in 83 percent of all consultations, the client never gets a second bid. In 68 percent of consultations, the client never even talks to a second consultant, meaning 68 percent of the work is awarded without the client talking to anybody else or getting any alternative bids. This amazes me as much as a similarly high number of people who will not shop two dealers when buying a car. Everyone thinks that people shop for cars. They do not. They go to the first dealer and buy a car. I would suggest that you do not go to the first consultant and buy consulting services without shopping around, and by this stage in the consulting process, ideally you will have searched and evaluated sufficiently to have found the perfect consultant for your desires and needs.

Summary

Taking the time and effort to evaluate the qualifications, capability, and suitability of potential consultants can be a daunting task, yet the results of careful evaluation—finding the right consultant for you—can be immeasurably valuable. As you have learned from this chapter, to discern whether a prospective consultant meets your needs, desires, and style, you need to:

1. Conduct a personal, face-to-face interview.

2. Ask essential questions to establish the consultant's qualifications:
   a. What does the consultant regard as your principal need or problem?
   b. What can he or she offer you that competitors cannot provide?
   c. How will evaluation of success take place?
   d. Will the consultant work on a performance basis?
   e. What experience does the consultant have working

with organizations similar to yours, or other organizations in the industry or field?

f. What experience does he or she have in working with needs and problems similar to yours?

g. Who are the consultant's references?

3. Discuss with the consultant the desired outcomes and expectations of the consultation.

4. Establish with the consultant measurable objectives for the consultation.

5. Discuss financial arrangements and contractual terms and conditions.

6. Assess your own fears—fear of consultant incompetence, continuing dependency—lack of managerial control, excessive fee, time availability, evidence of failure, disclosure of proprietary information, improper diagnosis/needs analysis, lack of impartiality—with the consultant, determining if they are increased or alleviated.

7. Alleviate the consultant's potential fears.

8. Check references.

9. Shop around. Do not hire the first consultant who seems to meet your needs without evaluating the competition.

Consider all these factors when evaluating your potential consultant. Most of all, listen to your gut feelings and instinct: if a consultant seems to have all the right answers, impeccable references, and excellent experience but you somehow feel he or she is not right for you, you are probably correct; if a consultant seems a little unsure, unpolished, and inexperienced, but you are convinced of the quality of his or her abilities and feel you would work well with this person, then you are also probably right.

7
The Consultant's Fee

No subject on consultants seems to evoke more curiosity than the matter of fees. At first glance, they seem high, or at least unpredictable and elusive. Clients frequently wonder if the daily charge of $500, $1,000, or $2,000 is plucked from thin air, and they worry about whether the consultant charges other clients less. Often, the corporate manager who receives a salary of $200 a day (about $52,000 a year) is repelled when hearing that a consultant charges $750 a day.

There are even jokes about the seeming irrationality of the consultant's fees. One of the more popular jokes involves two consultants talking to one another about fee-setting strategy. The first reveals his strategy to the second by saying, "I tell the client that the fee for my services is $250. If the client shows no sign of surprise, I add 'per hour.' If, on the other hand, the client looks shocked, I say 'per day.'"

But despite such jokes, the fees most consultants charge their clients is really quite logical and, in most cases, reasonable. In this chapter and the following two, I explain how consultants normally determine their fees and explain them to the client.

What Do Consultants Charge?

This little-understood area of consultant fee setting primarily involves two issues: 1) What do consultants charge? and 2) How do consultants choose to disclose their fee information with the client?

Each year, I conduct a nationally based research project on the economics of consulting to determine, among other things, how much money consultants are making, how they are spending their time, and their daily billing rate. The results of this research are published in my monthly newsletter, *The Professional Consultant and Information Marketing Report.*

The most recent research findings demonstrate that the average daily billing rate for all consultants in the United States and Canada is $977 a day. This is a median figure, so half of the consultants charge more and half of the consultants charge less.

Certain fields of consulting are more highly compensated than others. For example, in engineering, we find that the average daily billing rate is $1,133 a day, substantially more than the average daily billing rate for consultants in general; however, in education it is considerably less—$706 a day.

Figure 7–1 indicates the median daily billing rates for consultants, by field of specialty, for the United States and Canada as a whole (Canadian figures have been adjusted to United States dollars reflecting the exchange rate as of March 31, 1989).

Median daily billing rates are an important statistic for evaluating the health of a consulting practice, but they do not always reflect the financial success of the practice. Data reveal isolated instances in which a daily (or hourly) billing rate is high, but consultant annual income is low by comparison. This phenomenon is often the result of the fact that the quoted fee rate is so high—in the minds of the clients—that the consultant is unable to sell many days (or hours) of time.

Daily or hourly billing rates can be misleading in another respect: some consultants quote a relatively high daily (or hourly) billing rate but actually charge their clients significantly less because they work on a long-term, fixed-price of fixed-fee contract. Thus, a better measure of financial success of a consulting practice is often the annual income earned by the consultant after business expenses, but before income taxes.

Figure 7–2 indicates the average annual income of consultants, according to field or specialty, after business expenses but before federal, state, and local income taxes.

The research results indicated in figures 7–1 and 7–2 were

obtained from 6,998 surveys of a random sample of 11,631 consultants drawn from a population of 80,113 based on compilation from directories, membership rosters, subscriber and customer lists, and other mailing sources. The survey included professionals practicing in the United States, U.S. territories and possessions, and Canada. Canadian dollar figures have been adjusted to U.S. dollars at the exchange rate that existed on March 31, 1989. The findings reported are significant at the .05 level.

Why Do Consultants Seem Expensive?

As you can see, consultants are well-compensated, but they will tell you they work very hard for the money they get. Even though a consultant may charge a client several hundred to several thousand dollars a day, there are many expenses of doing business, not the least of which is the cost of downtime. Not every day is a billable day.

Though many consultants charge $1,000 to $1,500 or $2,000 a day, there are numerous consultants who charge $500 a day or $300 a day or less. Those charges seem expensive to a client who is hearing the number, especially for the first time. The reason consultants seem expensive is that the client is paying for a number of different costs: a salary to the consultant, fringe benefits to the consultant, overhead of the consultant—including the office, telephone, time spent in marketing and professional development/renewal, etc. All these costs add up, and the consultant is running a business, so you are also paying the consultant a profit on the running of his or her business. All in all, a considerable amount of money. It remains to be seen, of course, whether consultants really are expensive, but certainly they seem to be. First we want to talk about exactly what the consultant's fee consists of, and then we shall talk about how that fee is disclosed to the client.

Daily Billing Rate

Not all consultants set their fees on the same basis. Some quote their fees on a fixed-price contract; some, of course, on an hourly

All Consultants	$ 977	($ 929)
Accounting	$ 958	($ 912)
Advertising	$1,056	($1,001)
Agriculture	$ 672	($ 629)
Aerospace	$1,094	($1,023)
Arts & Cultural	$ 668	($ 644)
Banking	$ 989	($ 922)
Broadcast	$ 877	($ 872)
Business Acquisition/Sales	$ 903	($ 846)
Chemical	$ 955	($ 923)
Communications	$ 725	($ 682)
Construction	$ 873	($ 850)
Data Processing	$ 961	($ 926)
Dental/Medical	$1,077	($1,049)
Design (Industrial)	$ 841	($ 788)
Economics	$ 983	($ 899)
Education	$ 706	($ 682)
Engineering	$1,133	($1,086)
Estate Planning	$ 868	($ 869)
Executive Search	$ 944	($ 859)
Export/Import	$1,026	($ 967)
Fashion/Beauty	$ 551	($ 546)
Finance	$1,030	($ 993)
Franchise	$ 961	($ 902)
Fund Raising	$ 759	($ 711)
Grantsmanship	$ 677	($ 628)
Graphics/Print Trades	$ 696	($ 655)
Health Care	$1,102	($1,024)
Hotel/Restaurant/Club	$ 798	($ 724)
Insurance	$ 730	($ 707)
International Business	$1,022	($ 980)
Investment Advisory	$ 892	($ 821)
Management	$ 985	($ 933)
Marketing	$ 988	($ 939)
Municipal Government	$ 735	($ 691)
New Business Ventures	$ 844	($ 789)
Packaging	$ 873	($ 818)
Pension	$ 863	($ 842)
Personnel/Human Resources Development	$ 809	($ 769)
Production	$ 936	($ 883)
Psychological Services	$ 676	($ 637)
Public Relations	$ 791	($ 752)
Publishing	$ 790	($ 786)
Purchasing	$ 897	($ 844)
Quality Control	$1,023	($ 982)
Real Estate	$ 755	($ 686)
Records Management	$ 604	($ 595)
Recreation	$ 656	($ 611)
Research & Development	$1,139	($1,043)
Retail	$ 842	($ 807)
Scientific	$1,172	($1,097)
Security	$ 791	($ 708)
Statistical	$ 735	($ 719)
Telecommunications	$ 944	($ 872)
Traffic/Transportation	$ 803	($ 758)
Training	$ 832	($ 790)
Travel	$ 638	($ 634)

Figure in parentheses is March 1988 median billing rate.

Figure 7–1. *Median Daily Billing Rate for Consultants by Specialty
March 31, 1989*

All Consultants	$ 96,001	($ 91,102)
Accounting	$ 99,887	($ 95,098)
Advertising	$ 98,776	($ 93,323)
Agriculture	$ 69,210	($ 66,622)
Aerospace	$ 99,122	($ 93,274)
Arts & Cultural	$ 56,780	($ 54,285)
Banking	$ 92,349	($ 85,234)
Broadcast	$ 92,987	($ 86,990)
Business Acquisition/Sales	$101,335	($ 96,299)
Chemical	$ 88,767	($ 85,887)
Communications	$ 65,396	($ 64,721)
Construction	$ 89,533	($ 84,236)
Data Processing	$ 84,778	($ 81,008)
Dental/Medical	$100,004	($ 92,985)
Design (Industrial)	$ 70,094	($ 66,776)
Economics	$ 95,550	($ 90,654)
Education	$ 60,341	($ 58,430)
Engineering	$101,042	($ 96,311)
Estate Planning	$ 84,668	($ 82,237)
Executive Search	$100,296	($ 95,988)
Export/Import	$ 96,113	($ 90,142)
Fashion/Beauty	$ 57,499	($ 57,505)
Finance	$102,318	($ 97,689)
Franchise	$ 93,612	($ 87,755)
Fund Raising	$ 70,320	($ 69,213)
Grantsmanship	$ 61,888	($ 58,984)
Graphics/Print Trades	$ 72,571	($ 70,418)
Health Care	$104,002	($ 97,977)
Hotel/Restaurant/Club	$ 72,235	($ 70,445)
Insurance	$ 73,266	($ 68,461)
International Business	$ 99,873	($ 94,332)
Investment Advisory	$102,641	($ 98,826)
Management	$ 96,112	($ 91,222)
Marketing	$ 95,874	($ 90,465)
Municipal Government	$ 73,090	($ 69,078)
New Business Ventures	$ 76,482	($ 70,120)
Packaging	$ 91,366	($ 85,556)
Pension	$ 93,734	($ 85,003)
Personnel/Human Resources Development	$ 71,889	($ 68,126)
Production	$ 95,999	($ 89,052)
Psychological Services	$ 83,108	($ 80,907)
Public Relations	$ 73,157	($ 69,199)
Publishing	$ 80,446	($ 79,727)
Purchasing	$ 86,500	($ 81,144)
Quality Control	$ 94,233	($ 87,863)
Real Estate	$ 84,007	($ 81,650)
Records Management	$ 79,659	($ 79,668)
Recreation	$ 65,222	($ 63,235)
Research & Development	$112,886	($106,143)
Retail	$ 73,369	($ 72,936)
Scientific	$113,740	($108,774)
Security	$ 87,668	($ 80,244)
Statistical	$ 80,762	($ 78,198)
Telecommunications	$ 94,447	($ 89,543)
Traffic/Transportation	$ 80,123	($ 76,200)
Training	$ 78,581	($ 75,733)
Travel	$ 72,473	($ 71,993)

Figure in parentheses is for 1988.

Figure 7–2. *Average (Mean) Annual Income of Consultants after Business Expenses and Before Income Tax, for the Twelve Months Ending March 31, 1989*

rate. However, almost all consultants base their fees on something we call the daily billing rate. The daily billing rate, which corresponds to the average figure of $977 mentioned in figure 7–1, is determined by adding together three separate and distinct charges:

1. A charge for the consultant's labor.

2. A charge for overhead, or the consultant's expense of being in business.

3. A charge for profit, which the consultant makes by being in business.

Daily Labor Rate

The daily labor rate equates to the value of the consultant's labor in an economic society. Whether the consultant is your employee or someone else's, or an outside, independent consultant, that person's labor has specific value in our society. In general, we may not know exactly what labor is worth, but once you have determined the necessary skills a consultant should have, you are in a better position to know the value of his or her labor because you know the specific task you want to accomplish. However, we are accustomed to thinking of the value of people's work in terms of yearly salaries: we think of someone as being a $30,000-a-year person, a $50,000-a-year person, a $100,000-a-year person. This is how our economic society tends to look at labor. To find out what a consultant's labor is worth on a daily rate basis, we have to divide the annual value of labor—the yearly salary—by the number of paid days in a year.

There are 365 days in the year. If we deduct 104 Saturdays and Sundays, there are 261 paid days in our society each year. Today, few people actually work 261 days. Some of that time is taken up by sick leave, some by vacation, some by holidays; nevertheless, in our economic system, people tend to be paid for 261 days a year. So if you bring in someone as your consultant who has the kinds of skills and talents that would normally result in that person having a gross annual income of $48,000, you would divide that $48,000 by 261 and would come up with $184—the daily labor rate. You have to pay someone $184 a day to get his or her salary up to $48,000 a year.

Overhead

Once the consultant determines the worth of his or her labor, he or she can then determine overhead costs. Almost all consultants in this country have an overhead rate between 65 percent and 145 percent of their daily labor rate. Larger consulting practices usually have higher overhead, but the average of all consulting practices in the country is about 88 percent. If a consultant has a $100-a-day labor rate, which would equal about a $26,000-a-year salary, and he or she has an 88 percent overhead, the consultant is going to charge $88 a day in overhead.

Profit

Once the labor rate and overhead charges have been determined, consultants add profit to the calculations of their total fee. Profit ranges from 15 to 20 percent of the subtotal of the daily labor rate and overhead. Here is an example.

Let us assume the consultant's daily labor rate is $340, roughly an $88,000- to 89,000-a-year person. If the overhead were 95 percent, which is about the norm, the consultant would add $323 a day to cover overhead. This brings the subtotal to $663, and if he or she elects to charge a profit of 20 percent on jobs, then he or she will add another $133 and arrive at $796. Now you have probably never had a consultant come to you saying he or she charges $796 a day for services. Instead, the consultant rounds the number—usually up, not down. Normally the number is rounded to the nearest $25, so a $796-a-day consultant becomes an $800-a-day consultant. Here are the figures in a more explicit and straightforward form:

$89,000 ...... Annual Salary

$340 .... Daily Labor Rate (annual salary divided by 261)

$323 .... Overhead (95 percent of annual salary, divided by 261

$663 .... Subtotal (daily labor rate + overhead)

$133 .... Profit (20 percent of subtotal)

$796 .... Daily Billing Rate (total of daily labor rate + overhead + profit)

$800 .... Rounded Daily Billing Rate (actual daily billing rate rounded to nearest $25)

Thus, if you wish to make use of this consultant's services, it will cost you $800 a day plus any direct expenses incurred on your behalf.

Cost Comparison with Staff Member

Do consultants cost too much money? To answer this, you must ask yourself how the cost of a consultant compares with the cost of a full-time staff member. Remember what you are paying for in a consultant. You are paying for:

Labor. There should be little or no difference between the labor rate a consultant charges and what you would pay a full-time employee.

Fringe Benefits. If you are a large organization, then you probably will find that your fringe benefits are higher than the consultant's fringe benefits;* therefore, it may be more cost effective, more economical, for you to go outside and make use of consultants because you will save on fringe benefits. However, consulting firms usually are small organizations—even many of the

---

*Large consulting firms may well have costs that equal or exceed yours.

largest are small organizations—and if you are a small organization, then you will probably find that fringe benefit expense is about the same.

Overhead. You must compare the consultant's overhead to your overhead. Does your overhead run approximately 90 percent of direct labor? You will find that for most industrial and commercial organizations, the overhead may be even higher than that, if you are fully costing out overhead. To fully cost out, you must consider the full range of expenses, including the cost of physical space an employee occupies.

Support. For the most part, when retaining a consultant, you do not need to supply certain support systems you typically provide for your own organization: secretaries, telephones, electricity, personnel administration, and so forth. Essentially, you do not have to provide a whole host of accommodations to the average consultant who comes to you as a total business entity.

We should point out, however, that some consultants work within the client's organization. Their fees are normally less than the fees of consultants who work wholly independently. Consultants working within the client's organization use the client's telephone, secretarial staff, office space, and so on. Consultants who do not maintain offices and who simply float from client to client should be less expensive than the consultants who have a fully burdened overhead.

Whether you employ a consultant who works out of your office or one who maintains a separate office with his or her own overhead, when you break down the expenses of employing someone, most organizations find that consultants generally are more cost effective than full-time employees. In fact, a number of organizations in this country and worldwide are now in some stage of converting certain full-time employees into consultants. Perhaps the largest and most notable example of this is Rank Xerox Corporation of London (see chapter 2). The organization terminates people as employees and sets them up as independent consultants. These new consultants are paid approximately the same salaries they received as full-time employees, but they now work out of their own homes or their own offices, reducing the firm's overhead costs considerably. Xerox provides computer terminals for interaction with the company and allows the consultants to work with other individuals or other organizations to build their consulting practices. For the same money, these people are now putting in two to three days a week for Rank Xerox, leaving them the rest of the week to expand and build their own consulting practice. This arrangement can be mutually beneficial for organization and employee.

Reduced complexity is another reason corporations and other organizations are turning toward the use of consultants. Employment of people can become a bureaucratic and legal hassle. It requires complex administration, and the freedom to terminate employees has become fraught with complications and complexities, not the least of which is the trouble and cost of dealing with former-employee litigation or answering inquiries of state and federal agencies. Because the consultant-client relationship is temporal and normally regulated by a specific contractual agreement, many organizations find the ease of working with consultants beneficial in terms of administrative stress, as well as cost.

Summary

Consultants' fees vary according to the changing economy, according to field, and perhaps most of all, according to individual. Consultants seem extremely expensive, but they seem much less costly when the fee is broken down into its various components, as it is in this chapter.

Most fees are based on a daily billing rate, which is broken down into separate costs:

Daily Billing Rate:

1. Daily labor rate—a charge for the consultant's labor, determined by taking the yearly salary and dividing it by 261, the typical number of paid days in the year.

2. Overhead—the consultant's cost of staying in business.

3. Profit—the amount of money (usually 15 to 20 percent of the daily labor rate plus overhead) the consultant makes by being in business.

And while consultants may seem costly to you even after you have a basic understanding of how they establish their fees and that you are paying for more than just a salary, in general they are more cost-effective and efficient than hiring and training full-time personnel.

8
How Consultants
Determine Overhead

I n chapters 6 and 7 we briefly discussed overhead and pointed out that the consultant's charge is for a daily labor rate, overhead, and profit. You probably want to know just what you are paying for in that overhead, so in figure 8–1 is an example of the overhead of a management consultant who charges $1,000 a day for services.

Daily Salary Requirement

The consultant in this example has a daily salary requirement, or a daily labor rate, of $350. He or she has a $90,000-a-year salary (261 days × $350 = $91,350). The consultant expects to bill clients fourteen days a month, or 168 days a year.

Remember, the full-time consultant does not serve or bill clients every day. There are approximately twenty-one working days each month. A full-time consultant rarely bills more than two-thirds of available time, unless, of course, the client insists on it. Clients have a way of insisting on rush jobs or have true emergencies, which often result in the consultant's working twenty-eight or twenty-nine days a month, but this is not normal or preferable from the standpoint of the consultant.

Typically, the consultant wants to bill fourteen days a month—this is what is known as a full load. The remaining seven days are usually spent by the consultant in such tasks as marketing his or her services, managing the consulting business, engaging in professional development/renewal, and taking vacation or sick leave.

Let us now examine the actual expenses of the consultant.

Daily Salary Requirement (Daily labor rate) of $350 ($91,350)
Expectation of billing clients fourteen days a month, 168 days a year

Category of Expense	Monthly	Annual
Secretary ($2,000 monthly)	$ 800	$ 9,600
Office rent	825	9,900
Telephone and postage	375	4,500
Automotive	300	3,600
Personnel benefits/Employment taxes	900	10,800
Equipment and supplies	200	2,400

Marketing
  Personnel $1,400
  Direct   525
	1,925	23,100

Practice management	700	8,400
Dues and subscriptions	75	900
Professional development	300	3,600
Business licenses and taxes	30	360
Insurance	50	600
Accounting and legal services	200	2,400
Miscellaneous	175	2,100
Totals	**$6,855**	**$82,260**

Overhead Rate: $82,260 divided by 168 = $490

Figure 8–1. *Overhead Breakdown*

Overhead Expenses

Secretary

The first expense of our consultant is for a secretary working about forty hours a week. The secretary is paid a salary each month of $2,000. You will notice, however, that the consultant has not charged the overhead budget for all $2,000, only for 40 percent of it, or $800. What happened to the other 60 percent of the secretary's salary?

Through experience, this consultant has found that the secretary spends about 60 percent of the available time working on behalf of specific client projects or accounts, so the client is billed directly for that time. It is not an overhead expense. Forty percent of the time, however, our consultant's secretary is not working directly on a client account, but instead is doing things like answering the phone, reconciling the bank account, grinding out marketing letters, and other office tasks. Forty percent of the secretary's time is time spent doing jobs that are not directly attributable to or capable of being charged to the client. So this time and money has to be treated as an overhead expense.

Rent, Telephone, Postage

The second expense our consultant has is office rent—$825 a month. The third expense is telephone and postage. The consultant actually pays more each month for telephone and postage than these figures reflect; however, this is the amount of telephone and postage charged to overhead. A good part of the consultant's telephone and postage expense is attributable to particular clients; therefore, the clients will be billed directly for such expenses.

Consultants differ in how they handle direct charges. Some consultants have extensive bookkeeping and operating procedures where they bill their clients for virtually every direct expense incurred: every photocopy, every phone call, every postage stamp (if possible) is assigned to a particular client and billed to the client. Other consultants have less elaborate bookkeeping and less complex operating procedures, and they generally treat such expenses as overhead.

Consultants who do not directly charge their clients for such expenses, or at least most such expenses, obviously have higher overhead. Consultants who directly charge clients for every photocopy and every postage stamp have lower overhead. There are no free lunches in consulting. As far as the consultant is concerned, there is only one person who pays the bills—the client. The client will pay for them directly or indirectly, but the client will pay. So it is simply a question of individual procedure, accounting, operating style, and sometimes it is the common practice in a particular field of consulting or a particular geographic area that determines whether the client will be directly or indirectly billed for expenses.

Our consultant in this example actually has a monthly postage and telephone bill of about $700, but is able to assign approximately 50 percent of it directly to the client; the balance is handled as overhead.

Automotive

Our consultant buys a car for business use and charges the monthly car payment to overhead. However, actual miles driven on behalf of the client are billed to the client. Automotive, then, is a joint expense; the overhead budget essentially takes care of buying the car, and per-mileage charge provides for its maintenance.

Personnel Benefits and Employment Taxes

Like all businesses, a consulting practice has the expense of personnel benefits and employment taxes. Because most consulting practices are small businesses, such expenses are lower than such expenses for large organizations; nonetheless, they can be considerable. Figure 8–1 reflects an expense of $900 per month. Typical of these types of costs are expenses for the consultant and any employees for paid vacation, paid sick leave, paid holidays, major medical insurance, pension plan, and employee taxes.

Of course, there is virtually no limit to the possible fringe benefits a consultant could provide for himself or herself and staff members. Some larger consulting practices even provide such benefits as paid sabbatical leaves. And the longer a consultant is in business, the more likely it is that those things that began as benefits or privileges begin to be perceived by staff members or the consultant as rights.

For all practical purposes, however, most consulting practices provide a rather modest menu of fringe benefits at reasonable cost. The fact that most consulting practices are small, lean, entrepreneurial businesses attempting to maximize profitability rather than to develop elaborate compensation packages probably contributes to the decision to provide few elaborate benefits.

Equipment and Supplies

In our example, the somewhat modest budget of $200 a month for equipment and supplies is typical of management consultants, yet that expense can be considerably higher if it includes computerization and computer use. Some consultants need to obtain and maintain sophisticated technical equipment and instrumentation to operate their specialized practices.

Marketing

Usually the biggest expense for a consultant is marketing, because it takes the consultant a certain amount of time each month to be able to sell his or her services. In the case of our example consultant, we see that marketing expense is divided into two categories—personnel and direct expense.

Personnel covers the time the consultant spends marketing services. Recall that our consultant has a daily labor rate of $350. This is the personal income (or salary) the consultant expects to earn each day. Our consultant spends four days a month selling, or marketing consulting services. Four days time at $350 is $1,400. That $1,400 goes to pay for the time the consultant spends marketing his or her services.

The direct expense of $525 pays for nonpersonnel marketing expenses. Perhaps the consultant takes an airplane trip to visit a potential client or must have a brochure typeset or printed; these, too, are marketing expenses. And perhaps the consultant publishes a newsletter to keep the marketplace informed of the consultant's existence, ideas, and approaches to problems. The cost of printing and mailing such a newsletter would also be charged to this direct marketing expense.

Normally the primary marketing expense of a consultant is the value of his or her time. Consultants do not usually engage in advertising; they do not expend funds on marketing activities that involve expensive printing or media budgets. Typically, 70 to 80 percent of the total marketing expense is tied up in the labor of the consultant. This involves not only initial meetings with a client, but time expended on such activities as needs analysis and proposal writing.

Practice Management

Our consultant has a business to run. If the consultant spends two days a month managing the business (at $350 a day), that is an expense of $700 a month for practice management. This cost can be more or less, depending on the time actually spent managing the practice and depending on how accurate the consultant is in figuring time into the overhead.

Dues and Subscriptions

To stay current in the field and to maintain professional relationships, consultants often are members in and pay dues to various professional organizations and subscribe to professional and technical publications; a budget in the overhead for dues and subscriptions provides for these expenses—in our example consultant's case, $75 a month.

Professional Development

The consultant also engages in professional development. He or she attends various seminars, conferences and meetings to stay current in his or her field. Besides the expense of the time spent doing this, the consultant also has direct expenses for seminar and conference fees, materials, and travel. To the extent that the consultant is practicing in a field that experiences rapid changes and advances, we can expect such costs to be higher than the norm. Having state-of-the-art knowledge and expertise is, after all, a consultant's stock and trade.

Business Licenses, Taxes, and Insurance

Different professions and branches of consulting require various business licenses and incur the added expense of taxes. Moreover, most consultants have some form of insurance for operating their practice; most have business liability insurance, fewer carry professional liability insurance. These expenses vary considerably from consultant to consultant.

Accounting and Legal Services

Like every business, our consultant needs, from time to time, the services of an accountant and a lawyer. This is not necessarily a regular monthly expense; however, the cost of counting and legal services is certainly added to the overhead.

Totals

Our consultant, then, has $6,855 a month in overhead expense to operate the consulting practice, or $82,260 a year. If we divide the $82,260 a year by the number of days the consultant expects to be billing clients—168 days a year—we find that the consultant must charge $490 for overhead for each billable day. If the consultant does not charge an overhead expense, he or she is going to lose money. The consultant's overhead, then, is $490 for each billable day.

Daily Billing Rate

Daily Labor Rate	$ 350
Overhead (140%)	490
Profit (19% of $840 ($350 + $490))	160
DAILY BILLING RATE	$1,000

(Hourly Billing rate = $125)

Because our consultant has a daily labor rate of $350 a day and an overhead rate of $490, his or her overhead is 140 percent. Mathematically derived, 490 is 140 percent of 350, and in the professional services, business overhead is always calculated as a percentage of direct labor.

If our consultant charges a profit of 19 percent, he or she becomes a $1,000-a-day consultant. If the consultant elects to charge by the hour, the consultant might say he or she is "$125 an hour." However, many consultants will charge more by the hour than the day. It would not be uncommon for our example consultant to say that the fee is $150 or even $200 an hour, or $1,000 a day. Nor is it uncommon for consultants to establish minimum billing times, to say, "I am $1,000 a day, with a minimum three-day assignment," or "I am $200 an hour, but there is a minimum of four hours."

It has been said by many clients, and perhaps quite accurately, that the greatest benefit from a consultant comes in the first hour, and after that it is all downhill. Probably it is not all downhill; however, it has always been my belief that consultants would benefit from charging $1,000 for the first hour and $50 for each hour thereafter.

This, then, is the daily billing rate or hourly billing rate approach. It is the most common way consulting services are sold. If you examined all agreements between clients and consultants you would find that about 40 percent of the time, consultants are working on an hourly or a daily billing rate with their clients. Consultants find it the easiest way to work because it means the consultants do not have to estimate very hard—they do not have to think about their charges very long. Moreover, the client is taking the risk. If the project takes twenty days, it takes twenty days. If it takes ten days, it takes ten days. The consultant will keep working as long as the job takes.

Clients, on the other hand, tend not to like daily rates as much. They want to know what their total dollar exposure is going to be. So clients like to ask for arrangements like fixed-price contracts for getting a job done. And consultants, recognizing this fact, have in recent years more often proposed working on a fixed-price contract basis. They have found it is easier to sell consulting services that way and it keeps their clients happy.

Is a Larger Practice More Cost Efficient?

A larger consulting practice or several independent consultants associating with one another can potentially spread overhead costs over a larger base. If I have five employees, I will have a different overhead rate. If I can spread some of the overhead over more people, I will bring the overhead rate down a bit—maybe. I am also going to increase the managing, though. In such a case, I am clearly not going to get by spending one or two days a month managing the practice. I probably will have to spend twelve days a month managing the consulting practice.

Go back and look at overhead. What overhead really goes down when you add more people? Not very much of it. Clerical work probably goes up because of increased in-office communication. More bureaucracy always leads to more documentation, so you are not going to save very much money. You are not going to save in office rent because people take up space, and you cannot put five people in the space in which you put one person. You are not going to save a great deal in telephone and postage because five people generate five times as many phone calls and five times as much mail. Automotive might go down because the employees probably will not be given a car. You will get a little bit better buy on personnel benefits, but you also will have a staff of five people agitating for more holidays, better insurance programs, etc., which will probably raise the cost of fringe benefits at some point.

You may, however, get improved marketing efficiency. This is where you will see the biggest savings in overhead. With practice management there will be no savings, and dues and subscriptions will probably not change much. Professional development may become a little more cost effective, but these are really about all the changes you will see. So you will not see a huge drop in overhead in a large consulting practice. The argument that a larger consulting practice is more cost efficient is not really very meaningful, and probably should not have much bearing in your decision to hire a consultant.

Summary

As you can see, overhead—a large portion of a consultant's fee—can be broken down into a number of expenses that vary according to individual consultants' needs.

Overhead typically consists of all or a percentage of the costs for:

1. Secretarial salary
2. Office rent
3. Telephone and postage
4. Automotive
5. Personnel benefits/Employment taxes
6. Equipment and supplies
7. Personnel and direct marketing
8. Practice management
9. Dues and subscriptions
10. Professional development

11. Business licenses and taxes
12. Insurance
13. Accounting and legal services
14. Miscellaneous

Consultants generally add together daily labor rate and overhead, taking a percentage of this subtotal—usually 15 to 20 percent—as profit and adding it to the subtotal; therefore, a consultant's daily billing rate is the total price of daily labor rate plus overhead plus profit.

Daily billing rate is the most common way consulting services are sold. It is also often divided and expressed as an hourly billing rate, and many consultants charge considerably more per hour than per day.

9
Disclosure of the Fee

As a client, you have some options in how you buy a consultant's services. There is the daily/hourly rate basis, as suggested in the previous chapter. There is the fixed-price basis, which is always preferred by clients because the client no longer takes the risk; the consultant takes the risk. There are also several risk-sharing arrangements, the most common being the fixed-fee-plus-expenses.

Beyond that, there are a variety of ways consultants and clients may agree to work. There are performance or contingency contracts, not-to-exceed contracts, cost-reimbursable contracts, fixed-price-plus-incentive contracts—whatever the two parties agree to is fine. But they need to agree to something.

Now a daily/hourly rate, as I have said, is probably the most prevalent consulting rate. However, the fixed-price contract is also common. When you use a fixed-price contract, the consultant is going to quote to you a firm dollar amount for getting the job done. I personally much prefer fixed-price contracts, and I do 85 to 90 percent of my consulting on a fixed-price basis. I like to be able to tell my clients exactly what it will cost them to accomplish the job; then it is up to me to deliver the job within the confines I have set. Ideally, that is what should happen when you hire a consultant at a fixed-price rate.

When a consultant works on a fixed-price contract basis with you, the consultant will have to carefully estimate the total costs that will be incurred to get the job done. To determine the fixed-price charge the client must pay, the consultant first estimates how many people will be needed to do the proposed assignment.

Direct Labor:				
Senior Professional	15 days ×	$250 =	$3,750	
Associate	10 days ×	175 =	1,750	
Secretarial	8 days ×	90 =	720	
				$6,220
Overhead:				
95 percent of $6,220				$5,909
Direct Expense:				
Air travel		$505		
Postage		120		
Rental car		80		
Printing		135		
Per diem		170		
R. Lottnoy, Ph.D.		900		
Auto mileage		50		
				$ 1,960
				$14,089
Profit (Fee):				
15 percent of $14,089				$ 2,113
Total Fixed Price				$16,202

Figure 9–1. *Consultant's Estimation Sheet*

The consultant's estimating sheet (which you normally will not see) probably looks something like the example in figure 9–1.

The consultant may first estimate it is going to take fifteen days of the consultant's senior professional time to accomplish the job. Let us say that in this case the consultant's daily labor rate (not billing rate) is $250 a day. Fifteen days times $250 is $3,750.

Further, to get this job done, let us say that the consultant is going to use an associate. The associate is always paid less, naturally, but the associate does earn $175 a day, and the consultant estimates the associate will work ten days on your assignment. Ten times $175 is $1,750.

The consultant's secretary will be involved for eight days on this assignment, and eight days times $90 a day is $720. Thus, we have total direct labor of $6,220.

After estimating direct labor costs, the consultant will add in overhead. If we suppose that the consultant's overhead is 95 percent, then take 95 percent of direct labor, which would be $5,909, and that is the amount the consultant will add for overhead.

The consultant must now estimate all direct expenses that will be incurred during the consultation. The consultant's reasoning might be something like the following: The assignment necessitates an out-of-town trip, and the consultant finds that the round-trip air fare will be $505. While the consultant is on this trip, a car will have to be rented, and let us say that is expected to run $80. When the consultant is traveling, he or she receives a per diem of $120 a day, which covers hotels, meals, and incidentals, and $50 for partial days because there is no hotel room. The consultant will be traveling for a day and a half, so $170 will cover per diem.

The consultant also knows that he or she will have to mail a survey instrument and figures postage will run $120. Printing the survey instrument and the final report will cost approximately $135.

When the consultant has to make a round trip out of town, he or she will spend half a day flying out and half a day flying back. Does the consultant bill this time to the client? The normal procedure is for consultants to directly bill travel time to the client, but many do not. Again, we get back to the notion that there are no free lunches. The client eventually will pay for all costs, either in the form of higher overhead or as a direct charge. My philosophy, and that of most consultants, is that a cost like travel time should be directly billed to clients because there are wide discrepancies in the amount of time a consultant will spend traveling for different clients. To charge local clients (through overhead) for travel time that you incur for other clients does not seem equitable. A consultant should treat an item as an overhead item only if it generally is about the same for all clients.

The assignment you want the consultant to complete may include tasks the consultant has no skills for or is not capable of doing, for example, statistical analysis of data. The consultant and his associate were never fortunate enough to have passed statistics, but their good friend down the street, Dr. Lottnoy, does do statistical consulting and charges $450 a day, so our consultant decides to subcontract part of this job to Dr. Lottnoy. Dr. Lottnoy will need two days, so that will cost $900. Then, at twenty cents a mile, the consultant expects that traveling around town getting the job done will cost $50 in automotive or mileage expenses.

Thus, the total direct expenses on this job, according to the consultant's estimates, are going to be $1,960.

When the consultant adds up direct labor, overhead, and direct expenses, the total comes to $14,089. If the consultant charges a profit of 15 percent, that is $2,113, rendering a total fixed price of $16,202. And the consultant will say to you, the client, "I will get the job done; I will make the problem go away for $16,202." That is a firm, fixed-price arrangement.

Some consultants argue that the assignment must be a routine type of job for the consultant to have enough understanding of the work involved to enable the completion of the work on a fixed-price basis. Like their clients, consultants have a certain aversion to risk. They worry about having an inadequate understanding of your full and total expectations and thus bidding the job too low. They fear that fully satisfactory (to you) completion of the assignment may involve spending more hours or days of time and more direct expenses than they estimated. Despite such concerns, which are legitimate, (and are often based on past experience of the consultants), the fact remains that much of the work consultants do not want to do on a fixed-price basis could be done that way if they were not so lazy at estimating.

The trick to being good at estimating is to break the job down into small, manageable areas. But people get lazy or they get busy, and sometimes they just do not want to go to the trouble of precise estimating. Yet experienced consultants have found and will continue to find that they will sell more consulting if they will simply go to the trouble of estimating and coming up with fixed-price bids. It is not that difficult to do, if the client is willing and can provide a clear definition of his or her needs.

If the consultant believes the client has not properly defined the job, problem, or scope of work, then it is the consultant's responsibility or obligation to point out errors he or she feels the client may have made and to discuss such matters with the client. There may simply be miscommunication between client and consultant, and there may indeed be a lack of understanding; these should be cleared up regardless of the method of fee disclosure.

If there is anything fundamental to the consulting process, it is frankness and open communication between consultant and client. Each party should feel free to press the other for information to encourage a spirit of cooperation and understanding.

Many consultants have discovered that through experience they have begun to know how much additional or undefined work can be expected from particular kinds of clients—how many extra meetings, how many extra reports, how many extra trips. So they often inflate their estimates a little to accommodate these expectations and still be able to work on a fixed-price basis. This is known as a pad. A true contingency is when the consultant comes to the client and says, "I believe I can get this job done for $16,202, but it will not exceed $20,000"—an almost $4,000 contingency.

As a client, you will normally prefer the fixed-price contract because, as I have said, you have no risk. You have a very simple decision here. Is it or is it not worth $16,202 to get this job done? If the value of getting the job done is worth $16,202 or more, you will say yes to the consultant, sign a contract, and the consultant will begin work.

Risks and Fears

Despite the value to the client of getting the job done, clients always tend to fear the estimate aspect of the fee. In a fixed-price bid, the fixed price is always an estimate, not an absolute. Suppose that when the consultant actually does the work, the project does not take fifteen days, it takes only thirteen days; the consultant's associate finishes in seven days, not ten days; the consultant buys an airplane ticket from some dying airline and flies round trip for $39, not $505. What has happened? The consultant has completed your assignment for less than the estimate. And the consultant is going to make more profit.

The client may say, "Your costs were less than you thought.

Why don't you reduce your fee?" The consultant is going to say, "No, it is a fixed-price contract. You agreed to pay me $16,202 for getting the job done." You see, the attitude of the consultant is that he or she was lucky and had an underrun, but it might well have been an overrun instead. Assuming your consultant is truly professional, if it took twenty days to accomplish the job, the consultant would have spent twenty days. If it took the associate fifteen days, the associate would have spent fifteen days. And if the consultant found the flight booked and wound up having to fly first class for $720, he or she would have paid that bill, too.

Consultants do not profit from every job. Obviously, they hope to profit from most of their jobs, but in our system of economy, the risk taker is the profit maker, and you cannot have it both ways. You cannot ask the consultant to take the risk on a fixed-rate basis and then reduce the fee if the consultant is more efficient or effective than he or she expected. But had this job been done on a daily-rate basis and the consultant spent five fewer days finishing the job, you would have saved money. It is all a function of who is taking the risk.

There is no way of really knowing whether you would have saved money on a daily-rate contract versus a fixed-price agreement. It could go either way. When you and the consultant decide how you will work together, each of you is really making the decision on the basis of your willingness to accept risk and uncertainty. I have been involved in many consultations where the client insisted on a fixed-price arrangement, where in reality the client would have saved money had the work been performed on a daily-rate basis. But these clients elected to minimize their risk.

Often if the quality of the desired result is crucial or of paramount importance, the client will find it most valuable and effective to work on a daily-rate basis with the consultant. It may be in the client's better interest to risk paying more and being assured of the quality of the result than to have to worry that the consultant might cut corners and come up with a less desirable result.

Clients and consultants should not approach their relationship as adversaries. They should be working toward the best outcome in a spirit of cooperation and trust. The client wants the project completed on time with state-of-the-art professional services. The consultant should want to do the best job possible and be compensated reasonably.

The fixed-price contract, then, has the consultant taking the risk. With a daily rate, the client takes the risk. To work on a fixed-price contract, the consultant must be able to estimate with accuracy direct labor and direct expenses. If the consultant feels the job is sufficiently unstructured or too open-ended or unpredictable, the consultant will not want to work on a fixed-price contract, simply because it is too risky. If you want consultants to serve you on a fixed-price basis, you will find it in your interest to define and delimit the jobs you want accomplished because the more structure you give the consultant, the more likely it is the consultant will be able to make accurate estimates and thus be able to work on a fixed-price basis.

Fixed-Fee-Plus-Expenses

Often a consultant can estimate direct labor but feels uncomfortable estimating direct expenses. For instance, the consultant does not know up front whether there will be one trip or three trips and whether the statistical analysis will take two days or five days. So if the consultant can estimate direct labor but not the direct expenses, then you will find that the consultant will probably want to work a fixed-fee-plus-expenses basis. The consultant gives a fixed amount for getting the job done, excluding direct expenses, and gives the client an estimate for direct expenses, but makes clear that the client will be responsible for the direct expenses, whether more or less than the estimate. The fixed-fee-plus-expenses contract is a risk-sharing arrangement between client and consultant. The consultant takes the risk on the labor component of the project, and the client takes the risk on direct expenses.

Thus, the most common way in which consultants bill services to clients is with a daily/hourly rate, the second most common is on a fixed-price basis, and the third most common is fixed-fee-plus-expenses. There are other arrangements into which consultants and clients may enter, as well. Further information about different types of fixed-price contracts and other fee arrangements are included in the next section.

More about Fixed-Price Contracts

Fixed-price contracts between client and consultant have two specific features: 1) The consultant is obligated to perform at the agreed price regardless of the costs the consultant incurs, and 2) The client is not obligated to pay anything to the consultant unless the consultant delivers that which has been agreed upon. In practice, however, clients often make partial payment for partial and/or incomplete work by the consultant.

Fixed-price contracts usually involve progress payments tied to the achievement of predetermined milestones or according to arbitrary predetermined dates. Technically, if a contract is not completed to the satisfaction of the client, monies paid in progress must be returned to the client.

The fixed-price contract limits or eliminates risk to the client and puts all risk with the consultant. In return for this risk, the consultant will receive a greater profit than the estimated profit if the work is more efficient, more effective, or more creative than the estimate suggested.

There are two keys to success in entering into fixed-price contracts: first, a precise and specific definition of the work or task to be performed and second, capability in making estimates. Either the client must make clear the specific tasks and assignment, or the consultant must become expert in extracting information from the client to enable construction of a precise task requirement.

In the case of contracts with the federal government and most states, the consultant is required to keep working until the government-client accepts the result. A major advantage of the fixed-price contract in government work is that the contract is not subject to controls on such things as labor rates, per diem rates, fees or subcontractors, and similar costs. There are several types of fixed-price contracts:

Firm Fixed-Price Contract

This is a firm fixed price or payment for specified work. It is not subject to change, adjustment, or negotiation, except formal negotiation resulting from a change in the scope or character of work to be performed. All risk lies with the consultant and the greatest opportunity for profit is made available to compensate for this risk.

Escalating Fixed-Price Contract

This is the same as the firm fixed-price contract except that it contains provisions for upward and/or downward adjustments of the fee on the basis of predetermined contingencies such as cost-of-living index. Because of high inflation in the current economic scene, this contract form is being used more widely as a protection to consultants engaged in extended assignments.

Incentive Fixed-Price Contract

This fixed-price contract contains what is known as "an adjustment formula" to reward the consultant for efficiency in the conduct of the consultation. A target cost and profit are established at the time the contract is signed and then are subject to later adjustment based upon actual performance. Such contracts normally contain a ceiling price that holds the consultant fully responsible for costs above a certain predetermined amount.

If the consultant estimated costs on the assignment to be $25,000 and desired a profit of $5,000, the contract price would be $30,000. If both parties agreed that additional expenses would be borne by the client at a rate of 75 percent and by the consultant at a rate of 25 percent, and actual expenses were $30,000 rather than $25,000, then the profit earned by the consultant would be $3,750 rather than $5,000. Profit is reduced by the 25 percent of the additional expenses which, by agreement, were the responsibility of the consultant. The client might also have placed a ceiling on allowable expenses. In this case, the consultant might be responsible for all expenses in excess of $35,000.

Performance Fixed-Price Contract

This is the same as a firm fixed-price contract except that a provision is made for some special performance by the consultant that will produce a higher-than-contracted-for profit. For example, the contract is for $9,000; however, if the consultant delivers the final output or product within forty-five days of the date of the contract, the consultant will be paid $9,750. An incentive for rapid delivery in the amount of $750 is planted by the client as a motivation tool for the consultant.

Fixed-Price Contract with Redetermination

This is the same as a firm fixed-price contract except that a provision is made that allows both the consultant and the client to redetermine or reset the price to be paid by the client after the contract has been signed. This contract is best used when the nature of the consultant's task is so vague, so uncertain, so unknown as to make an estimate impossible or almost impossible.

At the time the contract is signed, the parties predetermine a milestone event in the project, at which point they agree to redetermine the basis of actual cost and expense experience. By agreement, the parties determine whether the change in price shall affect prior work, future work, or both. The contract is usually in the interest of the consultant, who is working on a blind or unknown task for which costs may be much higher than anyone would have conceived. But redetermination may be downward, too. If actual costs are a great deal less than anticipated, this contract may not be to the advantage of the consultant.

Time-and-Material Contracts

Time-and-material contracts result in the consultant's being paid for actual labor expended plus overhead, cost of materials, and a handling charge for the materials. When a consultant works on a daily rate plus expenses, the contract is very close to a time-and-materials contract.

The time-and-materials contract places all risk on the client and none on the consultant. As a result, consultants frequently prefer this type of contract relationship with clients. It is often advisable and indicated if the client is unable to be specific about the tasks to be performed. Most consultants find that experienced clients prefer fixed-price contracts to time-and-materials contracts. Time and materials really provide an incentive to the consultant to be anything but efficient. The more time charged, the more money made.

The consultant usually establishes a daily rate, hourly rate, or weekly rate. This rate combines a charge for labor, a charge for overhead, and a charge for profit. The client is charged for the actual amount of time expended on the basis of the unit rate being charged. The consultant also charges for all expenses (materials) in connection with the client's job at their actual cost plus a handling fee. The handling fee is most frequently a percentage amount—equal to the percentage of profit charged on labor—added to the expense.

Support services (for example, clerical assistance) are usually charged as an expense, but if the amount of such support services can be determined with relative certainty in advance, they may be added into the daily or hourly rate. In such cases, the daily rate is called a "fully burdened (daily) rate."

In one sense, time-and-materials contracts are fixed-price contracts. The labor rates and overhead rates are fixed. But the total dollar expenditure by the client is anything but fixed.

Cost Reimbursement Contracts

Cost reimbursement contracts are founded on the basic assumption that the client pays all costs or the consultant ceases performance. The contracts generally are used in situations where accurate estimates are improbable or impossible and where the cost accounting system of the consultant is adequate to enable monitoring by the client. For obvious risk factors, clients usually do not desire this type of contractual relationship with consultants. Where such contracts are used, clients usually expend substantial effort to ensure an adequate system of surveillance so as to eliminate wasteful practices on the part of the consultant.

This general type of contract usually involves a determination of so-called "allowable costs." This concern is particularly important when the client is a government agency. Certain kinds of costs—for example, cost of capital—may be viewed by the consultant as reasonable, but be viewed by the client as not allowable. When entering into this kind of contract, make a clear predetermination of what shall constitute allowable costs.

A cost reimbursement contract is rarely appropriate in a price competition award.

Several types of cost reimbursement contracts are used:

Cost Contract

The client agrees to reimburse the consultant for all allowable costs but pays no fee. This form is most widely used when the consulting agency is nonprofit and when the consulting agency will learn technology that will enable it to profit in future activities. It is also possible to have what is known as cost sharing. In such a case, the client agrees to reimburse the consultant for a part of the cost.

Cost-Plus-Fixed-Fee Contract (CPFF)

The CPFF contract is the most frequently used form of a cost reimbursement contract. Its popularity in general consulting developed as a result of its widespread use by the federal government. The client and consultant agree on the total estimated cost of the consultation or project and further agree as to the allowable fee or profit to be earned by the consultant. If actual costs are lower than those estimated, the consultant will earn a higher percentage fee on the costs. If the original cost estimate was $100,000 and the fee $20,000, that is a total compensation of $120,000 to the consultant; however, if the costs only run $90,000, the rate of return on costs earned by the consultant will be 22 percent rather than 20 percent. Yet if the costs are higher than estimated, the consultant does not earn any additional fee, and the rate of return will be less than estimated.

The theory behind the CPFF is that the consultant will be motivated to keep costs down to earn a higher percentage return. In practice, however, this is not always the case. The consultant is largely assured of reimbursement for all "allowable" costs and normally not required to spend funds in excess of the agreed-upon amount, even though the project or consultation has yet to be completed.

Cost-Plus-Incentive-Fee Contract (CPIF)

The CPIF is similar to the CPFF but is designed to provide greater cost saving motivation for the consultant. Rather than a fixed fee, this contract form has a minimum fee and a maximum fee. The minimum fee may be negative or zero. In short, the consultant is rewarded by a greater dollar fee if the costs are less than estimated and receives a smaller fee or no fee if the costs are greater than estimated. Frequently, CPIF contracts involve multiple incentives: for example, an incentive based on cost efficiency plus an incentive based on completion. As with the CPFF, the CPIF can involve cost sharing.

Consider the following possibility. The target estimated cost on the project is $10,000, and the target fee negotiated between the consultant and the client is equal to $2,000. Further, the parties agree to share costs in excess of target costs on a ratio of 70/30. That is, the client will be held responsible for 70 percent of the costs in excess of the target and the consultant for 30 percent. The parties also agree that the consultant will receive an incentive equal to 25 percent of the value of any cost underrun. Now, if the actual costs on the consultation or project are $7,000, the consultant will receive $2,000 plus 25 percent of the $3,000 underrun—or a total of $2,750.

Had the costs been $12,000, the consultant would have been responsible for 30 percent of the cost overrun of $2,000, some $600 of which would have been deducted from the profit of $2,000, yielding a profit to the consultant of $1,400.

While each party attempts to obtain an advantage during the course of contract negotiations, the theoretical concept on which a CPIF contract is based is that the probability of either a cost overrun or underrun is equal.

Cost-Plus-Award-Fee Contract (CPAF)

This contract is a cross between the cost-plus-fixed-fee and the cost-plus-incentive-fee contracts. It was first used in the federal procurement process to handle technical procurements of a nature too difficult to estimate and to provide a reliable basis for contract negotiation. The minimum or maximum fee is on the basis of an evaluation, often by an external and independent person or group, as to how cost effective and compliant the consultant was. There is no requirement that the evaluation take place at the end of the consultation. Often evaluations are scheduled on a monthly or quarterly basis. One advantage of frequent evaluations is that they provide feedback to the consultant, which may prompt performance more in line with the client's expectations.

Retainer Contracts

While the term "retainer" is used in many different ways, the classical usage of the term implies an open-ended type of agreement between client and consultant to make the consultant available to the client for a specified amount of time or scope of work. Usually, additional work is billed out at some preestablished hourly or daily rate. From the vantage of the consultant, the retainer contract makes good sense only when the consultant is able to predict with strong accuracy the amount of time that will be spent in meeting the client's objectives. In the absence of a strong estimate of the amount of time, the consultant is largely limited to the retainer agreement that simply guarantees that a certain amount of hours will be expended on behalf of the client. From the client's standpoint, a retainer agreement is of value because the client has the ability to tap quickly and with ease the specialized talent of the consultant without a great deal of formality in the engagement process.

The use of an Availability Retainer Agreement has become more common in recent years. This is a special type of retainer in which the consultant simply makes himself or herself available in the event that the client needs the consultant's services. The consultant agrees to reserve a specified block of time for the client in the event of need. As this reduces the time flexibility of the consultant, the consultant is rewarded a portion of the value of the reserved time. Most often this amounts to a sum of between 20 and 30 percent of the value of the time.

If there is a change in the scope of the work, then the fee may be redetermined and the contract renegotiated. The consultant probably will be sure that this happens. The client may forget that he or she just added another two hundred hours worth of work, but the consultant will be alert to that fact and will not let such changes go undocumented.

Performance/Contingency Contracts

In a performance/contingency contract, the consultant is paid on the basis of quality or quantity of performance consultant produces. There are fundamentally two situations when a performance contract is used. One is when the consultant perceives a high economic gain from his or her efforts and desires to participate in that gain. The other situation is when the consultant perceives there is a resistance on the part of the client in wanting to work with the consultant—lack of faith in the consultant's skills, perhaps. As a result of the client's lack of confidence, the consultant will propose working on a performance basis so as to reduce the risk the client perceives.

The consultant's attitude and perception of high gain is that he or she should be compensated for making the client some money. For example, I know of consultants who are hospital cost-recovery consultants. Their clients are major hospitals that have been unable to recover all the money believed to be due them by insurance carriers and government agencies, and the consulting firms fight for the client's money. They receive 30 percent of everything they recover for their hospital clients. Each year, they recover millions of dollars and receive 30 percent of those millions—a very profitable consulting practice. Their clients pay on a basis of performance.

The client's attitude and perception about a performance contract is to let the consultant take the risk. The client's risk is virtually eliminated because the consultant must satisfactorily accomplish the job if he or she wishes to be paid.

To have a performance contract, you must have measurable outcomes. A performance contract is an agreement that says that we will define some measurable criteria, some performance. Measurable outcomes are specifically defined, observable, measurable results, as we have discussed earlier—dollar profit, actual dollars of sales, reduction in kilowatt hours used, and so forth.

In addition, if you expect the consultant to work on a performance contract basis, you must give the consultant control over the resources that will produce the performance. Do not ask consultants to jeopardize their economic interest by not allowing them to control those resources.

I had a client who had a new product called a Widget and who wanted me to do a direct-mail promotion. It was a client I had worked with a couple of times previously, but not for about two or three years.

The client wanted me to market the new product through direct mail and wanted me to develop the marketing and promotion system, working on a performance basis—the client would pay me 37 cents for every Widget sold. However, once we got down to specifics, it turned out that I would not be given control over all the resources. The client wanted to reserve the right to select the mailing lists, or at least approve what I selected; the client wanted to reserve the right to change or modify my promotional brochure—and so on. I told the client I would be happy to do the job but said I could not work on a performance contract basis because while I might design the world's greatest brochure, the client might select an inappropriate and undesirable mailing list and I would not make any money. If the client wanted to pay me on the basis of my performance, it had to be willing to put me—not someone else—in control of the criteria that would affect my performance.

That is why performance contracts are infrequently used: clients usually are not willing to relinquish control over the resources that will, in fact, produce the desired performance. Performance contracts, incidentally, usually wind up costing you, the client, more. They have a higher dollar compensation than any other kind of contract, for if you are asking your consultant to take risks, the consultant expects to be well compensated for taking those risks.

Consultants and clients get together because, in their mutual understanding and estimation, their working together will produce a desirable result for both. It will give the consultant income, and it will solve some problem or accomplish some need of the client. In most consultant-client relationships, the objective of getting the job done properly and adequately is more important than anything else. If, because of a lack of understanding or unforeseen circumstances, modifications and adjustments have to be made, most of the time consultants and clients will agree to make the necessary changes, even if there is an additional fee required to accomplish the changes, because the objective is getting the job done. A good consultant does not have making money as his or her objective. A good consultant's objective is serving the client. Making money is the measure of the consultant's success, but it is not the purpose for which someone goes into consulting.

Summary

When client and consultant decide to work together and agree upon the means of payment, each makes the decision on the basis of his or her willingness to accept risk and uncertainty. There are many fee arrangements: some place most of the risk on the consultant, others put most of the risk on the client, and still others divide the risk between client and consultant. Among the types of fees and contracts are the following:

1. Daily/hourly fee—Client takes the risk

2. Fixed-price fee—Consultant takes the risk
   Fixed-fee-plus-expenses—Shared risk
   Escalating fixed-price
   Incentive fixed-price
   Performance fixed-price
   Fixed-price with redetermination

3. Time-and-material contracts—Client takes the risk

4. Cost reimbursement contracts—Client takes the risk
   Cost contract
   Cost-plus-fixed-fee

Cost-plus-incentive-fee
Cost-plus-award-fee

5. Retainer contracts

6. Performance/contingency contracts—Consultants takes the risk

10
The Proposal

I would recommend that the client be convinced in the initial interview—and it may be the only interview—that the consultant is competent. Then, if you are convinced of the consultant's competency and think that you may wish to retain his or her services, ask for a project proposal. The proposal should be written because it is extremely important for a client to know how well a consultant writes. The consultant may be very articulate verbally, but how are his or her writing skills? In so much of what most consultants do, writing ability has a strong impact. It should reflect an ability to organize and manipulate data, to deal with complex situations, ideas, and information, and to conceive of and express appropriate and innovative ideas to respond to a problem.

You may, and should, certainly ask for written proposals from more than one prospective consultant to decide who will ultimately be best suited for your job. In the proposal, the consultant should express his or her understanding of the problem and/or the client's needs; state the ways in which the consultant plans to solve the problem and fulfill the needs; set goals and define specific, definite, measurable, and obtainable objectives; establish a time frame for the project; suggest how and when progress reports and evaluations will be made; and calculate costs of the consulting services and determine a method of payment. Of course, depending upon the size, scale, and extent of your project, the proposal can be more or less detailed and extensive to suit your particular needs.

I have a client in Chicago that is a large company, and through the years I have done work for several different divisions of this particular company. Once I was asked to go to Chicago to discuss a new project. The meeting lasted four and a half hours. The decision to retain my services was what you might call a "committee decision," as there were three or four different units within this division participating in the discussion. When I left that meeting, my responsibility was to submit to them a proposal based upon our discussions and verbal proposals. Over the next week I prepared a proposal; they approved the general scope of services and entered into a contract for $54,000 of consulting services. Two weeks later we met in Los Angeles for two purposes: to let me observe one of their activities, changes in which would be part of my responsibility during the consultation, and to sit down and make a few amplifications and/or corrections to my original proposal.

The point is that the client felt sufficiently confident to go ahead and enter into the contract before the proposal was revised, assuming that I would not mind making a few corrections or changes. Often a sophisticated client will work in this fashion. Such clients know that a major benefit of using consultants is the flexibility that can be created. But open communication must be set up and maintained. I might well have misinterpreted what they said to me in Chicago, or they might well have changed their minds once they saw their objectives and my ideas in writing, or they might have changed their minds just because of a change in business circumstances or conditions. Here we see a case where there was nothing more than a first meeting proposal before acceptance. Then there have been other situations I have been involved in where multiple meetings and changes have taken place before a contract is signed.

The written proposal can take the form of a formal proposal or a less formal letter proposal. The letter proposal lacks the strict organization and structure of a formal proposal, but it must be carefully written to cover major points and answer questions the client might have. As in most letters, brevity is the key to success; however, the proposal still must be as specific as possible. Every word and phrase should be chosen with care to have the maximum effect. The letter proposal should contain an outline of the steps and goals in the project, a time-line of milestones in the projected, and a description of the consultant's fee. You, the client, can ask the consultant for such a proposal if it is suited to your needs, or you can ask for a more formal proposal; it is up to you.

The Formal Proposal

The written proposal is an important part of the consulting process. It shows the client what is needed and how the consultant can supply what is necessary to fulfill the needs. If the sale has already been closed, then the proposal is an outline of the project and is not an attempt on the part of the consultant to emphasize the qualities that would convince a client to sign.

The proposal should be developed only when both consultant and client believe that a good opportunity for success justifies the expenditure of time and effort. The proposal must communicate the consultant's ideas so that the reader (the client and decision maker) is convinced the consultant can achieve what he or she proposes within the quoted budget estimate or fixed price.

The consultant must convince the client that the need for the consultation is important. This involves showing that not implementing the consultation will harm the client's interests, and that the consultant's goals and objectives will correct the problem and take care of the need. The client must be convinced that the procedures the consultant proposes are the best and are only alternative for taking care of the problem or need.

The proposal is divided into three sections: the front, the main, and the conclusion.

The Front Section

The front section communicates the consultant's understanding of the purposes of the consultation and the needs it is intended to fulfill. If you, the client, have sought the services of the consultant, then the consultant will show his or her understanding of those needs. If the consultant seeks to inform the client of the need for using his or her services, the consultant must show how those services will benefit the client and what consequences may develop for the client if the consultant is not retained.

The front section will establish objectives and goals that will direct the services the consultant will deliver. Goals are statements of broad direction or intent. Objectives are specific statements of outcome presented in a format that will enable the client and consultant to determine when they have been met. This section also establishes a mandate for action, such as compliance with existing or expected laws, cost effectiveness, warding off adverse publicity, increased profits, and so on.

The front section usually includes the following:

1. A letter of transmittal
2. The proposal cover
3. The proposal title page
4. An abstract
5. A table of contents
6. A statement of assurances
7. A statement of need
8. A statement of objectives

Letter of Transmittal

In addition to indicating that the proposal is being delivered to the client organization, the letter of transmittal also conveys the consultant's availability and high level of commitment to the proposed project.

Cover

Since it is what a client looks at first, the cover should be of professional quality, reflecting the quality of the proposal and the consultant's services. While appearance is not everything, it can give you some indication of how the consultant does business; a sloppy cover may indicate sloppy work.

Title Page

The title page may include limitations on distribution.

Abstract

The abstract is a one-page, single-spaced summary of the project proposal—brief and to the point.

Table of Contents

The table of contents is a road map through the document. It should make the reader want to go on by arousing interest in the same way newspaper headlines do.

Statement of Assurances

The statement of assurances can communicate that:

- The proposal is, in the consultant's estimation, as cost effective as possible consistent with the client and project's needs.

- There are no lawsuits or judgments pending against the consultant.

- The consultant does not discriminate in hiring.

- The consultant self-insures, holds the client blameless, and will defend any lawsuits.

This statement should be dated and signed by the highest official of the consulting practice.

Statement of Need

The statement of need is one of the two most important parts of the front section. It enables the reader—the client—to independently assess the extent and validity of the needs the proposal addresses. In the statement of need, the consultant should describe the problems in terms that are meaningful to the client. The consultant should also avoid the use of soft terms such as "a substantial number," "a high degree," and "a downward trend," instead, using hard and quantifiable terms that are as specific as possible.

Statement of Objectives

The statement of objectives is the second of the two most important parts of the front section. Each objective the consultant formulates must convey some specific information to the reader. Each objective should:

- Describe the outcome the consultant intends to produce.

- Provide a means of measuring the results.

- Set the level or quality of outcome necessary to carry out the project.

The Main Section

The main section contains the functional flow diagram (FFD), a time-line communicating when the work should be/will be done, and a written narrative explaining the results and benefits to be achieved by each activity outlined in the FFD.

The functional flow diagram is a pictorial description of the entire scope of activities the consultant can perform for the client. It is made up of a series of lines and boxes. A label is attached to each box, with each box representing a major component of project activity; the label is usually descriptive of one or more activities that may go on within the box.

The time-line gives dates or periods of time needed to complete each stage of the project. The time-line can be expressed as a line with the dates and project stages marked on it. The time-line need not detail exactly the time between events; however, it should be in order and should leave sufficient time for the necessary client reviews and approvals.

The written narrative communicates the outcomes, results, and benefits of the consultation to the reader. It shows how the FFD will achieve the objectives and communicates the fact that you, the client, will have the opportunity to manage the consultant. For each activity/box in the FFD diagram, there should be a one- or two-paragraph statement about the activity and a general description of how procedures will be employed. The consultant's written narrative should be specific enough to communicate to the client the type of work the consultant will be doing; however, an experienced consultant will make it general enough to prevent the client from taking the consultant's work and getting a free or lower cost consultation.

The Proposal Conclusion Section

The concluding section may include the following, although not every proposal will require all of these elements:

1. An evaluation plan and procedures
2. A reporting and dissemination plan
3. A consultation/project management and organization plan
4. A consultation/project price/bid
5. A consultation staff statement of capability

Evaluation Plan and Procedures

Many consultations will involve a distinct evaluation of the work done for the client. This is particularly true when the consultant performs a creative or technical task such as auditing, market research, training program design, information system design, etc.; it is also quite common in all government work.

Evaluation provides a check or measurement of the quality of the consultant's work and the viability of the specific plan/procedures the consultant is proposing. It is a means by which the client can hold the consultant accountable for the expenditure of funds.

A properly designed project/consultation evaluation is really like a separate and distinct consultation. Indeed, the evaluation is often given to another consultant to complete. In such cases, the evaluation is then said to be an "independent" or "third party" evaluation. Even if the consultant and client are not planning to conduct a formal evaluation, the consultant should indicate that an ongoing or in-process evaluation will be conducted and should describe the various activities that will take place. You, the client, will gain confidence by knowing that a continuous monitoring is under way to assure quality control.

Reporting and Dissemination Plan

The written final report has become commonplace for many client organizations. It may call for up to one hundred or more copies to be disseminated.

Consultation/Project Management
and Organization Plan

The project management plan contains information that enables the client to assess the consultant's qualifications to be awarded the contract. The plan must show that the consultation will be conducted by individuals who have an understanding of client needs and who can work with the client's administrative structure. The management plan also demonstrates that the consultant has management and administrative skills, as well as creative ideas. Many people are creative, but they have trouble getting results because they are poor managers.

The management plan should describe the administrative structure of the project, including:

- A detailed list of any key positions and associated responsibilities and duties.

- A description of the connective link between consultants working on the project and the client's organization.

- Estimates of personnel the consultant anticipates will be needed to complete the project (a personnel loading analysis).

- A description of the background and qualifications of personnel who will be assigned to the project.

- A description of any outside individuals or organizations needed to carry out the project, if necessary.

Personnel Loading Analysis

The personnel loading analysis gives the distribution of work hours or days for each element of the project. If the consultant finds that certain elements require too many personnel or hours, he or she may reorganize the time-line to spread out the functions more evenly over time. The analysis is typically used only in larger consultations involving a number of personnel.

Consultation/Project Price/Bid

The fee or bid is most often introduced in the proposal at this point. However, depending on the distribution of the written proposal, the consultant instead may include the price/bid in a confidential letter delivered separately from the proposal. If so, the prospective client will indicate to whom the price/bid should be sent.

Consultation Staff Statement of Capability

The statement of staff capability usually includes the resource-sand talents of the consultant organization and the specific resumés of key personnel who will contribute to the client's project. The consultant's brochure will usually serve as an adequate description of the consulting organization. For individuals involved, standard resumés should suffice.

Assessing the Proposal

It is up to you, the client, to assess the proposals you receive and decide which proposal, which consultant, which bid best suits you and your needs. You can ask that the proposal be as formal or informal as you wish; it can include as many or as few of these possible proposal components as you feel will give you an adequate understanding of the consultant's qualifications, operating style, suitability for the project, and ability to achieve success and fulfill your needs and goals. As well as the content of the proposal, the proposal's appearance can reveal something about the consultant. Good quality cover stock, paper, and binding gives the consultant a professional appearance. A proposal should not appear lavish and wasteful because it may indicate a consultant who will not be cost-efficient with your money; however, it should look professional, to (ideally) match the abilities of the consultant and the quality of the proposal.

Some sample proposals follow.

The first example is a brief letter proposal, containing an outline of the steps and goals in the project and a skeletal timeline. The fees are listed on a fixed-fee basis and there is a provision for charging for direct expenses and excess time spent on the project. Flexibility is introduced by giving the client a range of choices in retaining the consultant's services for all or part of the proposed project.

The second example is a letter combining a proposal and contract. This letter proposal/contract gets right to the heart of the matter and dispenses with legal formalities. However, it does constitute a binding legal contract if accepted by the client. Usually it is better to keep the proposal and the contract separate, but sometimes this approach is appropriate and useful. Such might be the case when the client has solicited a consultant of known reputation for a relatively short assignment.

Sample Proposal

Date

Name
Company
Address
City/State/Zip

Dear _____,

I enjoyed our telephone conversation of _____. AAA has an excellent marketing opportunity for its video seminars as public seminar programs and this letter is designed to serve as a proposal to define the steps I believe should be undertaken to evaluate and capitalize on the marketing potential. When we spoke, I had only received the video introduction, leader guide and participant materials for _____. Following our conversation, I received your letter of _____ and enclosures. The enclosures were particularly beneficial in the preparation of this proposal and I apologize for taking your time on the telephone to answer questions that were handled by the enclosures.

In my estimation, the decision of how to distribute should be based upon a recognition that AAA brings to the market for distributors a significant and very valuable asset. Accordingly, the analysis of options should carefully determine the market value of the programs to ensure that the full profit potential be realized. Careful attention needs to be given to potential outside distributors relative to such factors as:

Market experience and capability;

Financial viability and resources;

Importance of the AAA opportunity to their business; and

Credibility and capability to perform at a high level.

I believe the following steps should be undertaken to evaluate and capitalize upon the marketing (as public seminars) of AAA seminars in general and _____, specifically:

1. Determine the relative advantages and disadvantages of self-distribution in comparison to obtaining one or more established distributors.

   This step would include a competitive analysis of distributors, a determination of their marketing capabilities and their financial viability/future plans. It would also include an estimation of expenses and revenues (a pro forma) for self-distribution and would evaluate various self-distribution models such as licensing, franchising, and establishing an independent dealer network. Particular attention would be paid to operating practices and distribution models of successful and less-than-successful operating practices, and distribution systems of established seminar companies, including such organizations as _____. Further, the evaluation would concentrate on emerging learning methods that may, in time, prove more efficient and effective than live seminars and the consequences such technological changes might have on AAA programs in general and _____ in particular.

2. Identify and select potential outside distributors.

   Step 2 would build on the work already accomplished in step 1 and would identify those organizations that might serve as a suitable distributor for AAA programs as public seminars in general and _____ specifically. The result of this activity would be to identify a list of candidate organizations that might be solicited by AAA for that purpose. It is anticipated that such candidates would include established seminar providers, as well as other organizations not currently involved in the seminar business with strong, related marketing capabilities, that would be in a position to serve as a viable distributor.

3. Establish requirements for performance by outside distributors.

   This step would establish minimum requirements distributors would have to meet to be acceptable to AAA and would be based on marketing and financial information gained about providers in general and candidate distributors as a result of the analysis undertaken in steps 1 and 2. It is anticipated that such requirements would be quite specific about the nature and extent of marketing effort to be provided by potential distributors to ensure that distributions proposals submitted in the future by such candidates could be adequately evaluated relative to self-distribution options.

4. Structure offering package to outside distributors.

   On the basis of minimum requirements for distributors established as a result of the completion of step 3, and the determination of the profit potential for self-distribution determined as part of step 1, the specific offer(s)/proposal(s) to be made to potential distributors would be developed.

5. Solicit outside distributors.

   Offer(s)/proposal(s) developed in step 4 would be forwarded to candidate distributors.

6. Review outside distributor responses.

   Responses received from interested distributors would be reviewed and acceptable respondents would be interviewed and evaluated.

7. Decide upon method of distribution/select outside distributor(s).

   Acceptable distributor offers/proposals (as modified as a result of step 6), would be evaluated and compared to self-distribution options and a final decision would be made about the distribution for _____, specifically, and perhaps for other AAA programs as well.

I believe that the above activities can be accomplished as quickly as follows:

February 16–March 6, 1987

1. Determine the relative advantages and disadvantages of self-distribution in comparison to obtaining one or more established distributors.

March 2–13, 1987

2. Identify and select potential outside distributors.

March 9–20, 1987

3. Establish requirements for performance by outside distributors.

March 9–20, 1987

4. Structure offering package to outside distributors.

March 16–27, 1987

5. Solicit outside distributors.

March 30–April 17, 1987

6. Review outside distributor responses.

April 13–24, 1987

7. Decide upon method of distribution/select outside distributor(s).

I would be pleased to provide my services to AAA on either a per-hour fee basis or on a fixed-fee-plus-expenses basis, as you determine to be in your best interest. Listed below is my estimate of the hours I would need to complete the above activities. Also, please find the fixed fee that would be charged for the completion of each activity. If it is your preference to work on an hourly fee basis, the charge would be _____ dollars ($_____) per hour.

1. Determine the relative advantages and disadvantages of self-distribution in comparison to obtaining one or more established distributors.
    Estimated number of hours 30–40
    Fixed-fee charge .... $_____

2. Identify and select potential outside distributors.
    Estimated number of hours 12–20
    Fixed-fee charge .... $_____

3. Establish requirements for performance by outside distributors.
    Estimated number of hours 10–15
    Fixed-fee charge .... $_____

4. Structure offering package to outside distributors.
    Estimated number of hours 14–19
    Fixed-fee charge .... $_____

5. Solicit outside distributors.

   Estimated number of hours 01–04

   Fixed-fee charge .... $_____

6. Review outside distributor responses.

   Estimated number of hours 10–30

   Fixed-fee charge .... $_____

7. Decide upon method of distribution/select outside distributor(s).

   Estimated number of hours 15–25

   Fixed-fee charge .... $_____

In addition to the above, AAA would be charged for direct expenses incurred for travel and nonroutine communications, if any. The above estimates are based upon a total meeting time with you or others you might designate in amount equal to fifteen hours. Should it become necessary to meet for a duration or frequency in excess of fifteen hours, additional meeting time would be billed at $_____ per hour. There would be no charge for the first twenty-five hours of travel time, if any.

There is no requirement on my part for AAA to contract for all of the services indicated above. If you prefer, they can be taken one at a time and you could reach a decision at each stage as to the wisdom of further retention of my services. In the event you find it advisable to contract for all or several of the services outlined, please understand that AAA would be provided with the right to terminate my services at any time during the course of the consultation.

I hope the above information is sufficient to meet your requirements. If I may provide further information please don't hesitate to let me know.

I look forward to the prospect of working with you on this very challenging project.

Personal regards,

_____

Sample Letter Proposal/Contract

Pursuant to our conversation of Sept. 24, 1980, the following is the proposal of _____ (hereinafter referred to as the Consultant) for establishing and operating a recruiting effort designed to acquire the services of a minimum of five qualified software engineers for _____ (hereinafter referred to as the Client):

Proposal

1. Scope. The plan involves the consultant's assisting the client with a thorough preparation of the positive aspects of living and working in Phoenix, Arizona; recruiting, interviewing, screening, and qualifying candidates; conducting personal interviews when applicable; establishing "prime candidate" status; presenting candidates for final approval; assisting in closing negotiations with successful candidates; and establishing start dates.

2. Plan & requirements. The consultant will develop a portfolio that will positively present all the client and the area have to offer.

   We will require a plant visitation. While there, we will require scheduled meetings with key personnel.

   You should have prepared:

   (a) Complete job descriptions for current recruiting assignments;

   (b) A complete statement of relocation policy or assistance program, as well as any contractual requirements in connection with these policies; and

   (c) A comprehensive explanation of wage, salary increases, benefits and advancement programs and schedule, as it applies or is required for the recruiting assignment.

3. Charges & terms. To accomplish all the above, the consultant will require a retainer in the amount of $5,000 per month for each of the two months covered hereby and a

like amount for each renewal month. The amount paid as a monthly retainer shall be applied against the service charge, as set forth below. For example, the service charge for the hire of an engineer is $9,000; therefore, the amount owed by the client will be $9,000 minus $5,000.

The recruitment cost for the hiring of software engineers each at an average salary of $30 per our regular service charge schedule (copy attached) would be $9,000. However, our quantity discount to you will reduce this amount.

The schedule is as follows:

1–2 engineers	Standard charge per engineer
3–5 engineers	15 percent discount per engineer
6–8 engineers	20 percent discount per engineer
9 or more engineers	25 percent discount per engineer

In addition to the professional service charge, we will expect the client to reimburse the consultant for reasonable and pre–approved expenses incurred in the course of this assignment.

Should the client terminate any employee hired through the consultant as a result of this assignment within the first ninety days of employment, the consultant will make every effort to replace the engineer at no additional charge to the client.

4. Term of agreement and cancellations. This proposal will be in effect for sixty calendar days from the date of receipt of the retainer and signed confirmation by the client. The consultant agrees to present to the client a minimum of eight qualified and prescreened software engineers during the period of the proposal, otherwise a prorated portion of the retainer will be refunded to the client.

   At the conclusion of said sixty days, the proposal may be renewed or extended by mutual agreement of the parties hereto.

5. The client retains the right of first refusal to all candidates recruited during the period of the proposal. At the conclu-

sion of the agreement, all candidates recruited by the consultant and not employed by the client or in the process of being employed by the client become the property of the consultant.

6. Consultant shall not, during the term of this agreement or afterward use or disclose to the client's detriment any confidential information whatsoever obtained from or through the client as a result of work done pursuant to this agreement, nor display for any purpose any drawing, letter, report or any copy or reproduction thereof belonging to or pertaining to the client without written authorization from the client, unless such drawings, letter, or report has been previously published by the client. The term confidential information used in this sub paragraph shall mean any device, process, method or technique originated by or peculiarly within the knowledge of the client, and its representatives, employees, and those in privy with it, which is not available to the public and is subject to protection as property under recognized principles.

7. The consultant shall not divulge without the permission of the client the terms and conditions of this agreement.

Either of the parties hereto may cancel this agreement on thirty (30) days' written notice.

If the above proposal is in accordance with your understanding of our agreement, please sign and return the enclosed copy of this proposal, along with the first month's retainer, to our office.

By _____

By _____

Dated _____

Summary

The written proposal is an essential part of the consulting process, outlining the consulting project. Proposals can be as formal or informal as need dictates, including as many or as few of the following provisions as desired:

Front Section:

1. Letter of transmittal
2. Proposal cover
3. Proposal title page
4. Abstract
5. Table of contents
6. Statement of assurances
7. Statement of need
8. Statement of objectives

Main Section:

1. Functional flow diagram
2. Time-line
3. Written narrative explaining the FFD

Conclusion Section:

1. Evaluation plan and procedures
2. Reporting and dissemination plan
3. Project management and organization plan
4. Project price/bid
5. Consultation staff statement of capability

The proposal should outline the project and convey a sense of the consultant's qualifications, creativity, innovativeness, operating style, suitability for the project, and—perhaps most importantly—ability to achieve success and solve the problem at hand, fulfilling your needs and meeting your goals.

11
The Contract

I always recommend that once you have decided to retain a consultant—you have some knowledge and understanding of your needs and expectations, the consulting process and consultants' fees—clients and consultants work with a written agreement. There are many advantages to a written agreement, but the main reason I recommend it is that it improves the quality of communications between the parties, ensuring a better and more cost efficient result.

So when negotiating a contract with a consultant, the client should always employ a basic strategy to achieve the following goals:

Avoidance of Misunderstanding

Misunderstanding by the client or client company is often caused by assumptions. When in doubt, the typical client often avoids asking the consultant for a full explanation and instead assumes the consultant's meaning. Thus, if the assumption disagrees with the real intent, trouble may ensue.

To avoid misunderstandings, I urge you to ask the consultant to spell out everything he or she intends to do—even the obvious. If the consultant does not volunteer in detail his or her intentions, try questioning the consultant about specifics and/or set down your own specifications for the project.

Assurance of Performance and Results

In order for you, the company, to have this assurance, it is necessary to be sure that the contract provides the following:

- A time schedule for the completion of services by the consultant, or a formula for determining such a schedule.

- A requirement for adequate insurance coverage. The client should be adequately protected either by insurance or by a hold-harmless agreement, or by both.

- A provision preventing the consultant (and the client) from assigning the contract or subcontracting a part of it without the written consent of the other.

- A provision giving the client the right to terminate the agreement if the consultant's performance is unsatisfactory or if the client has no further need of the services provided, or, in some cases, any time at the option of the client.

- By specific contract provision, a requirement that only competent personnel may perform or continue to perform work for the company. The company may want to request the assignment of a specific person or persons to perform the services, with identification of same in the contract.

- Requirements that the consultant obtain any necessary approvals by government agencies, that the consultant maintain adequate records, that the consultant make periodic reports to the company, and that any fee paid for a preliminary report to the company may be applied to the total fee for a completed project.

Components of a Contract

I. Preamble Section

The beginning of the contract merely sets forth the mutual intention and purpose agreed upon by you and the consultant in undertaking the agreement. For example, this is a typical preamble shell:

This agreement is entered into this _____ day of _____, _____, by and between (name of your company), hereinafter referred to as the company, and (name of consultant), hereinafter referred to as the consultant.

Witnesseth, whereas the company and the consultant are desirous of entering into an agreement for the purpose of:

(List Project Goals)

II. *Project Approaches*

This section typically involves a description as to how the two parties have agreed to accomplish the project goals set forth in the preceding section. It is the section that specifies the means to accomplishing the desired end.

Now, therefore, it is mutually agreed that:

(Description of how objectives will be accomplished)

A particularly useful insertion here is a reference to the written proposal, and in connection with which this contract is being drawn. The following is suitable wording for such an insertion:

The development and conduct of the project shall be as described in the project prospectus submitted by the consultant to the company on (insert date). The relevant descriptions from that document are attached hereto as Attachment "A," and are thereby incorporated into this document.

III. *Consultant's Tasks*

In this section of the contract you itemize the specific tasks for which the consultant is responsible. It is customary to preface each numbered paragraph of this section with the phrase "The Consultant will" or "The Consultant shall."

A particularly useful entry in this section provides for the consultant's continuing work with the company. For example:

The Consultant will regularly consult with the designated Company personnel for the purpose of monitoring and assessing progress, and to formulate indicated program changes so as to more effectively achieve the program objectives as formulated in attachment "A" (or other identifying symbol of the attachment containing the proposal materials.)

If you want the consultant to submit a final report, indicate that in this section, too.

> The Consultant will furnish to the Company on or before (insert date) a reproducible copy of the project final report. This report will include program materials and descriptions of all relevant aspects of program activity.

The services to be provided by the consultant should be set forth in sufficient detail to make clear the consultant's undertaking. Since trouble is being taken to develop the contract document, it makes little sense to be terse. The best advice is to leave nothing to question. Enumerate all the consultant's tasks and major subtasks.

A statement of the detailed scope of services to be provided by the consultant may include office consultations, field investigations and studies based thereon, preparation of reports involving feasibility, economic analysis, designs and plans, assistance in procurement and in making contracts with others, supervision of work on the project involved, inspections, costs, evaluations, and—finally—agreement for assistance in any litigation that might arise pursuant to the project.

IV. Company's Tasks

This section of the contract draft is similar to the previous section; however, it covers what you, the client, will do. You will find it helpful to designate one technically cognizant individual to act for the company in all technical matters pertaining to the contract. In this way, you are assured of a consistent interpretation of the contract terms and language.

V. Special Conditions

This section may be nonexistent in your contract, or it may be substantial, depending on you and your needs and the measure of precaution you wish to take. There are contingencies that can and do arise for which the contract should offer guidance. Consider, for example:

1. What happens if the company's funds are withdrawn?

2. What about failure or bankruptcy of the company or consultant?

3. What should be done in the case of nationwide strike or revolt, making it impossible to meet contract terms?

4. What should be done in the case of a natural disaster that destroys intermediate project accomplishments?

5. What about fraud or embezzlement leading to insolvency of either party?

VI. *Payment of Consulting Fees*

This section often begins with the phrase:

> In consideration of the satisfactory performance of the consultant, the company agrees to reimburse the consultant on the following basis:

It is important that the wording that follows this phrase be very specific. In this section, you should spell out the exact terms and conditions that will result in your meeting your milestones and achieving your results as you render payment to the consultant. If payment is to be made on a performance basis, great care must be taken to spell out the criteria of performance. Criteria of performance should be observable, measurable, evident, and obvious to the client, the consultant, or any other party.

The times and conditions of making payment should be set forth in sufficient detail to avoid any misunderstanding.

VII. *Option to Amend the Contract*

In the event of changed circumstances, or if the parties desire to change their agreement, a written amendment of the contract may be in order. If the changes desired are very extensive, it is often preferable to completely rewrite the contract as a new document.

Formal vs. Informal Contracts

For a client and a consultant to work together, it is not absolutely necessary to have a formal, legal contract drawn up by an attorney. A signed letter detailing the project—its components, its conditions, expected results, fees, etc.—can serve just as well. Whether you choose to have a formal document or simply a letter of agreement, make the terms and conditions of the consultation as specific, straightforward, unambiguous, and detailed as possible to avoid any misunderstanding between you and the consultant, so that your needs and requirements will be successfully and satisfactorily met. And if you choose to write a letter of agreement instead of a formal contract, it is never a bad idea to have it checked by an attorney as an added precaution. The more candid and straightforward the client and consultant are with each other, the more precautions you take to protect yourself (and the consultant) and ensure that the job will be successful, the more likely it is the consultation will be a mutually valuable, beneficial, and fruitful experience for both client and consultant.

The following section contains sample contracts and letters of agreement—both formal and somewhat informal ones.

Sample Contracts

When one party does not wish any written agreement, it may still be possible for the other party to supply persuasive evidence of their agreement by writing a letter. This letter should set forth the essential elements of their verbal agreement and request a reply if it does not accurately reflect the agreement of both parties. Either the client or the consultant may prepare the letter of agreement.

Sample Letter of Agreement 1

[Client's Letterhead]

Date

Name of Consultant
Address
City, State, Zip

Dear _____:

We are pleased to inform you that we have selected you as a [type] consultant to work for us on [specify project or nature of work] on the following terms:

1. Term. This agreement will be for an initial period of [specify, for example, two years], commencing on _____, 19XX, and may be extended for an additional period by mutual agreement in writing. This agreement may be terminated at any time by either of us by [specify, for example, giving thirty (30) days' written notice to the other party].

2. Duties. Your duties will include [specify, for example, the rendering of consultation and management services in connection with [name of project]]. You will consult with our Board of Directors, officers, and department heads concerning the organization and fiscal policy of our company. You will further have complete authority and power over the management of [project], including direction and supervision of the administrative staff. You may at your discretion arrange to assist in management duties and may delegate to staff such duties as you may deem proper.

3. Hours. You will devote a minimum of [specify how many] hours per month to your duties under this agreement, and you may, if you desire, devote any additional time. You are free to represent or perform services for any other

clients, provided it does not interfere with your duties under this agreement.

4. Compensation. For your services you will receive a reasonable monthly sum that shall be at least [specify] dollars ($_____) per month but that shall not exceed [specify] dollars ($_____) per month. We will pay you on the fifteenth (15th) of each month an amount mutually agreed on for services rendered during the preceding month. If we fail to agree on the amount to be paid for any given month, we shall pay you the minimum compensation provided and submit the dispute to a panel of three (3) arbitrators, one chosen by each of us and the third chosen by the other two, and their determination shall be final and binding.

5. Assignment. Because of the personal nature of the services to be rendered, this agreement may not be assigned by you without our prior written consent, but, subject to the foregoing limitation, it will insure to the benefit of and be binding on our respective successors and assigns.

If this agreement meets with your approval, please sign and return the original and one copy of this agreement, you may retain the additional copy for your own records.

Very truly yours,

[Signature]
[Typed name and title]

Accepted this _____
day of _____, 19XX
[typed name of consultant]

Sample Letter of Agreement 2
[Consultant's Letterhead]

Date

Name of Client
Address
City, State, Zip

Gentlemen:

Engineering Services

Report on [name of project] System

Submitted herewith is our proposal for services in connection with an engineering study and report on [name of project] system.

The engineering study and report will include the following items:

1. General field examination of the system.

2. Preparation of base map showing the location and size of [major items in system].

3. Analysis of system based on current volume and estimated future growth.

4. Recommendations for general development of system, including observations regarding alternative possibilities for future system development, including:

   a. System [volume].
   b. Number and general location of [outlets].

5. Establishment of priorities for necessary work to bring system up to ultimate design condition.

6. Estimates of probable investment required for initial improvements, together with maps showing initial improvements to system.

7. Estimates of probable investment required for future improvements, together with maps showing ultimate system layout.

8. Comments on condition and practices of present system and recommendations on improving conditions of present system.

9. Comments on generally accepted practices of [components], construction, and maintenance.

10. Comments on [type of equipment] and recommendations, with cost estimates, on necessary rehabilitation or replacement of existing gear. Recommendations to include ratings and general arrangement of major components of plan offered.

A written report will be prepared and presented in person to you. This report will summarize our findings and recommendations, which will serve as the basis for determining appropriations necessary for required facilities.

The report will be presented to and discussed with you within approximately [number] days after acceptance of this proposal.

It is understood that you will make available to us all plans, records, and other pertinent information from your files that will be of assistance to us in our work and will also provide the services of a [type of employee] to assist us during the time required to make the field examination of the system.

Our fee for the services outlined above will be [specify fee], which will be due and payable on presentation of the report.

This letter may be made a contract on your approval by affixing the date of acceptance and the appropriate signature in the space below.

Respectfully submitted,

[typed name of engineers]

By [signature]
[typed name and designation of person signing]

Accepted this _____
day of _____, 19XX
[typed name of client]

By [signature]
[typed name and designation of person signing]

Samples of the Formal Written Contract

As with the letter of agreement, the formal written contract may be prepared by either the client or the consultant. Review of the general form of a specific contract by competent legal authority is recommended for both parties, as is recommended for letters of agreement, too.

This form constitutes an agreement between consultants and their clients governing a complex business transaction to be undertaken by the client but with detailed advice and supervision to be provided by the consultants. The consultants not only advise the client on the proper method of carrying out the project involved, but also are given specific management authority over most aspects of the project. This type of situation may be necessitated by the requirements of a third party, such as a lender or lessor, who believes the services of the consultant are necessary to the successful operation of the project involved.

Provision is made for compensation of the consultants based on the amount of work they perform, with a minimum and maximum dollar amount of compensation provided for each month. The consultants also agree to provide a minimum number of hours of service to the client and that any additional time spent shall be at the sole discretion of the consultants. If disputes arise under the agreement, provision is made for arbitration in accordance with the rules of the American Arbitration Association. To protect the reputation and good name of the consultants, the contract contains a provision declaring the uniqueness of the services to be provided by the consultants and the irreparable harm to them that would result if such services were not fully performed. It provides that equitable remedies, including injunction and specific performance, may be obtained by the consultants if the contract is breached by the client. In this situation, the main force of this provision is to ensure that the consultants will continue to manage the client's project so that the third party investor may be fully protected.

Business Consultant and Management Agreement

Agreement made this _____ day of _____, 19XX, between [name of client] _____ (e.g., a Delaware corporation), hereinafter referred to as the "Corporation," and [name of consultant(s)] (both jointly and severally), hereinafter referred to as the "Consultants;"

Recitals

The Corporation is negotiating [description of project, e.g., to build or lease and to conduct and operate a general hospital] at the following location: _____.

It is the desire of the Corporation to engage the services of the Consultants to perform for the Corporation certain functions in the management and operation of [e.g., the hospital] and to consult with the Board of Directors and the officers of the Corporation and with the administrative staff concerning problems arising in the fields of [e.g., hospital management; fiscal policies; personnel policies; purchases of equipment, supplies, and services]; and other problems that may arise from time to time, in the operation of [e.g., a general hospital].

Agreement

Term

1. The respective duties and obligations of the parties hereto shall commence on the date [e.g., that the Corporation enters into said lease].

Consultations

2. The Consultants shall make themselves available to consult with the Board of Directors, the officers of the Corporation, and the department heads of the administrative staff, at reasonable times, concerning matters pertaining to the organization of the administrative staff, the fiscal policy of the Corporation, the relationship of the Corporation with its employees or with any organization representing its employees, and in general, concerning any problem of importance concerning the business affairs of the Corporation.

Management Authority of Consultants

3. In addition to the consultation provided for in paragraph 2, the Consultants shall be in complete and sole charge of the administrative staff of [e.g., the hospital]. The administrative staff of [the hospital] shall include all the employees of the Corporation directly, or indirectly engaged in the affairs of [the hospital] other than the Board of Directors of the Corporation, the president, vice-president, secretary, and treasurer of the Corporation, and [the medical] staff of [the hospital]. The [medical] staff is defined as those persons who [are licensed by the State of Delaware to perform, and are performing, services as physicians, surgeons, nurses, physiotherapists, social workers, psychologists, psychiatrists, pharmacists, and other services of a professional standing in the healing arts and sciences].

Management Power of Consultants

4. The business affairs of the Corporation that affect directly or indirectly, the operation of [e.g., the hospital], and which arise in the ordinary course of business, shall be conducted by the administrative staff. All members of the administrative staff shall be employees of the Corporation; however, the Consultants shall have sole and complete charge of the administrative staff, and shall have absolute and complete authority to employ (on such terms and for such compensation as they deem proper), discharge, direct, supervise, and control each and every member of the administrative staff. It is the intention of the Corporation to confer on the Consultants all powers of direction, management, supervision, and control of the administrative staff that the Consultants would have if the members of the administrative staff were direct employees of the Consultants.

Business Manager

5. The Consultants, in their sole discretion, may employ, in the name of the Corporation, a business manager. If such a business manager is employed, he shall act as administrative assistant to the Consultants and as the chief administrative officer of the administrative staff. The business manager shall be under the direct control and supervision of the Consultants. The Consultants may, from time to time, delegate to the business manager as much of the Consultants' authority as they deem proper with respect to the employment, discharge, direction, control, and supervision of the administrative staff, and the Consultants may withdraw from said business manager, at any time the Consultants deem it expedient or proper to do so, any portion or all of the said authority theretofore conferred on the business manager.

Fiscal Policy

6. The Corporation recognizes the necessity for a sound fiscal policy to maintain and promote the solvency of the

Corporation. To this end, it is hereby agreed by the parties hereto that the Corporation will establish reserve accounts for the following purposes:

a. A reserve account for the payment of any and all taxes that may be charged against the Corporation by any governmental jurisdiction.

b. A reserve account for the payment of all sums withheld from the salary or wages of employees of the Corporation and for which the Corporation is chargeable under the laws of any and all governmental jurisdictions.

c. A reserve account for the payment of all obligations due [name of lessor] pursuant to the terms and conditions of the above-referred-to lease.

d. A reserve account for the purchase of equipment necessitated by the wearing out or obsolescence of the equipment in use, or by the development of new equipment.

e. A reserve account for building maintenance and for expansion of physical facilities. The Consultants shall, from time to time, advise the Board of Directors of the amounts of corporate funds that should be deposited in each of said reserve accounts. This determination on the part of the Consultants shall be based on the principles of sound business management and the availability to the Corporation of said funds. The Corporation agrees to deposit corporate funds in said reserve accounts pursuant to the recommendations of the Consultants, and the amounts recommended by the Consultants. The reserve accounts shall be deposited in one or more national banks, or branches thereof, located within [county and state]. All checks, drafts, or other instruments by which funds are withdrawn from said reserve accounts, in addition to any other signature that may be required, shall bear the signature of one of the Consultants.

Consultants to Act As Agents

7. From time to time, the Corporation may deem it advisable to enter into agreements with [e.g., insurance companies,

prepaid medical plans, and other firms and associations which pay all or part of the expenses incurred or to be incurred by the hospital patients for the care and treatment afforded them while patients in the Corporation's hospital]. Consultants shall be the exclusive agent of the Corporation for the purpose of negotiating the terms and conditions of said agreements. However, Consultants shall not bind the Corporation to said agreements without first obtaining approval of terms of said agreements from the Board of Directors of the Corporation.

Authority to Contract

8. From time to time, the Corporation may wish to expand the physical facilities of [type of facility] or remodel or modify same. If costs to be incurred by the Corporation for such expansion, modification, or remodeling are less than $_____, Consultants may contract for performance of same in the name of the Corporation under the authority given them in paragraph 4 above; however, if such expansion, modification or remodeling is to be of such extent that the cost to be incurred by the Corporation for the performance thereof is $_____ or more, then the terms and conditions of said contracts for said expansion, modification, or remodeling shall be negotiated by the Consultants, and the Consultants shall be the exclusive agents of the Corporation for said purpose, but the Consultants shall not bind the Corporation to said contracts without first obtaining approval of terms and conditions of said contracts from the Board of Directors of the Corporation. The provisions of this paragraph shall apply with equal effect to the purchase of equipment and supplies.

Employment of Certified Public Accountants

9. It is understood and agreed by the parties hereto that services to be performed by the Consultants do not include auditing of books of the Corporation or of [name of project], preparing of any financial statements, preparing of

any tax returns or other documents required to be prepared by any governmental body having jurisdiction to tax, or any other acts or services normally performed by public accountants. The Consultants may engage, hire, retain, and employ, in the name and for the account of the Corporation, one or more, or a firm of, certified public accountants to perform for the Corporation the services denoted above in this paragraph. Said accountant or accountants may be employed, hired, engaged, and retained on such terms and conditions and for such compensation as the Consultants deem reasonable. [E.g., It is understood by the Corporation that the Consultants are partners of a firm of certified public accountants known as [name of firm]. It is specifically agreed that the Consultants may be, and the Consultants are, hereby authorized to employ said partnership, or its successors in interest, to perform for the Corporation the services denoted above in this paragraph, and the Consultants may obligate the Corporation to pay to said partnership, or its successors in interest, a reasonable amount for the performance of said services.]

Employment of Assistants

10. If it is reasonably necessary for the Consultants to have the aid of assistants or the services of other persons, companies, or firms to properly perform the duties and obligations required of the Consultants under this agreement, the Consultants may, from time to time, employ, engage, or retain the same. The cost to the Consultants for said services shall be chargeable to the Corporation and the Corporation shall reimburse and pay over to the Consultants said costs on demand.

Limited Liability

11. With regard to the services to be performed by the Consultants pursuant to the terms of this agreement, the Consultants shall not be liable to the Corporation, or to

anyone who may claim any right due to his relationship with the Corporation, for any acts or omissions in the performance of said services on the part of the Consultants or on the part of the agents or employees of the Consultants, except when said acts or omissions of the Consultants are due to their willful misconduct. The Corporation shall hold the Consultants free and harmless from any obligations, costs, claims, judgments, attorneys' fees, and attachments arising from or growing out of the services rendered to the Corporation pursuant to the terms of this agreement or in any way connected with the rendering of said services, except when the same shall arise due to the willful misconduct of the Consultants, and the Consultants are adjudged to be guilty of willful misconduct by a court of competent jurisdiction.

Compensation

12. The Consultants shall receive from the Corporation a reasonable monthly sum for the performance of the services to be rendered to the Corporation pursuant to the terms of this agreement; however, in no event shall the compensation paid to the Consultants by the Corporation be less than $_____ per month nor more than $_____ per month. The Corporation and the Consultants, by mutual agreement, shall determine the compensation to be paid the Consultants for any particular month by the fifteenth (15th) day of the next succeeding month. The final determination of the monthly compensation shall be based on the reasonable value of the services rendered by the Consultants, and within the range prescribed above in this paragraph. If the Corporation and the Consultants fail to agree on said compensation within the said fifteen (15) days, the amount of monthly compensation due the Consultants shall be determined by arbitration pursuant to the provisions of paragraph 14 below. Anything contained in this agreement to the contrary notwithstanding, the minimum monthly remuneration

of $_____$ shall be paid to the Consultants on the first day of the month of each and every month during the term of this agreement and the acceptance of said minimum amount by the Consultants shall not in any way diminish, affect, or compromise their rights to additional compensation as provided for herein.

Minimum Amount of Service

13. The Consultants shall devote a minimum of $_____$ hours per month to the affairs of the Corporation. Anything to the contrary notwithstanding, the Consultants shall devote only so much time, in excess of said $_____$ hours, to the affairs of the Corporation as they, in their sole judgment, deem necessary; and the Consultants may represent, perform services for, and be employed by such additional clients, persons, or companies as the Consultants, in their sole discretion, see fit.

Arbitration

14. Any controversy or claim arising out of or relating to the compensation to be paid by the Corporation or the Consultants for the services rendered by them pursuant to the terms of this agreement shall be settled by arbitration in accordance with the rules of the American Arbitration Association, and judgment on the award rendered by the arbitrator or arbitrators may be entered in any court having jurisdiction thereof. Any party to this agreement may submit to arbitration any said controversy of claim.

[The following paragraph may be used when more than one consultant is a party to the agreement.]

Failure to Act by One Consultant

15. It is understood and agreed that any direction or consultation given or service performed by either one of the Consultants, pursuant to the provisions of this agree-

ment, shall constitute the direction or consultation or the performance of service of both of the Consultants. If, for any reason, one or the other of the Consultants is unable or unwilling to act or perform pursuant to the terms of this agreement, such event shall not void this agreement or diminish its effect, and the performance on the part of the other consultant shall constitute full and complete performance of this agreement on the part of the Consultants.

Legal and Equitable Remedies

16. Due to the uniqueness of the services to be performed by the Consultants for the Corporation, and due to the fact that the Consultants' reputation in the community as business managers may be affected by the financial success or failure of the Corporation in the operation of [the project], in addition to the other rights and remedies the Consultants may have for a breach of this agreement, the Consultants shall have the right to enforce this contract, in all of its provisions, by injunction, specific performance, or other relief in a court of equity. If any action at law or in equity is necessary to enforce or interpret the terms of this agreement, the prevailing party shall be entitled to reasonable attorneys' fees, costs, and necessary disbursements in addition to any other relief to which he may be entitled.

Right to Manage

17. Except as specifically provided to the contrary herein and to the greatest degree allowable under the Corporation Code and other laws of the State of Delaware, it is the intent of the Corporation to confer on the Consultants the exclusive and absolute right to manage and direct all the business affairs of the Corporation that in any way concern the operation of [project] and that arise in ordinary course of business of [project]. Should any one or more of the provisions of this agreement be

adjudged unlawful by any court of competent jurisdiction, the remaining provisions of this agreement shall remain in full force and effect. Further, should one or more of the provisions of this agreement be adjudged invalid by a court of competent jurisdiction, such determination shall have no affect whatsoever on the amount or amounts of compensation to be paid to the Consultants pursuant to the terms of this agreement.

Governing Law

18. This agreement shall be binding on and shall be for the benefit of the parties hereto and their respective heirs, executors, administrators, successors, and assigns, and shall be governed by the laws of the State of Delaware.

Executed at [name of state] on the day and year first mentioned above.

Client
[typed name of client]

By [signature]
[typed name and designation of person signing]

Consultant
[typed name of consultant]

[signature]
[typed name and designation of person signing]

Form of Agreement for Technical Services

A typical contract for the delivery of technical consulting services is illustrated below. This basic format is typical of contract forms used by engineers, architects, educational consultants, design consultants, marketing consultants, and so forth.

This constitutes a formal contract for complete engineering services on a major project. It will minimize subsequent disagreements and constitutes compelling evidence as to the agreement of the parties if legal controversy should arise. The agreement contains recitals indicating the background. In the illustrated form, a preliminary engineering report has been made on the project to be undertaken. It is therefore possible throughout the form to refer to this preliminary report in connection with the services to be provided. The engineers agree to represent the client in all engineering matters involved in the project. It should be noted that the consulting engineers, although independent contractors, not only act as advisors on engineering matters, but also are required to take affirmative action in implementing the client's project. Except for a few specialized types of advisors, who might better be called analysts, it is usual for consultants/advisors to come up with a concrete work product helpful to clients in addition to merely telling the client what action to take. For example, an attorney advises on the possible provisions to be inserted in a will and on their legal effect, but the attorney does not leave the drafting and execution of the will to the client; instead, he or she produces a formal document called a will and arranges for its proper execution.

The main promise made by the client is to pay the consultant. Many bases of compensation are possible. In this sample contract, an example is given for compensation based on a percentage of cost excluding engineering and legal fees, land and right-of-ways, and the client's overhead. Such an arrangement is sometimes used in contracts with certain government agencies, although such a basis of compensation is sometimes made illegal because of temptation to the contractor to increase costs to increase his or her fee. In this agreement, such objection is partially overcome by providing that the percentage of compensation is reduced as the amount of cost increases. The form also provides compensation on the basis of employees' salary plus a fixed percentage of such salary. Such an arrangement is subject to the same objection mentioned before. Provision is made for payment to the consultants of specified percentages of their compensation as various stages of the work are completed. The agreement provides for additional compensation to the consultants if changes in plans and specifications are made after they are approved by the client. The standard per diem charge of the consultant will be used to determine the additional compensation.

Engineering Service Agreement

Agreement made this _____ day of _____, 19XX, between [name of client], hereinafter referred to as the "Client," and [name of consultant], hereinafter referred to as the "Engineers."

Recitals

The Client now owns and operates [type of structure].

The Engineers have heretofore prepared and submitted to the Client a report entitled "[e.g., Preliminary Report, (name of project)]."

The Client desires to retain the Engineers to provide complete engineering services on the project.

Agreement

It is hereby agreed that the Client does retain and employ the said Engineers to act for and represent it in all engineering matters involved in the project. Such contract of employment will be subject to the following terms, conditions, and stipulations.

Conditions of Agreement

Scope of Project.

1. The scope of the project shall include the improvements recommended in the [e.g., Preliminary Report, (name of project)] as prepared by the Engineers.

Plans and Specifications

2. The Engineers shall prepare such detailed plans and specifications as are reasonably necessary and desirable for the construction of the project. The specifications shall

describe in detail the work to be done, materials to be used, and the construction methods to be followed.

The Engineers shall obtain approval of the plans and specifications from [e.g., State Department of Health].

Duplicate copies of plans and specifications shall be submitted to the Client.

Advertisement for Bids

3. After the Client has approved the plans and specifications, the Engineers shall assist in the preparation of notice to contractors and shall provide plans and specifications for prospective bidders.

Awards of Contract

4. The Engineers shall have a representative present when bids and proposals are opened, shall prepare a tabulation of the bids and shall advise the Client in making the award. After the award is made, the Engineers shall assist in the preparation of the necessary contract documents.

Resident Inspection

5. The Engineers shall furnish competent resident engineers or inspectors to supervise the construction of the work. Said resident engineers or inspectors shall be assigned to the project during such periods as are mutually agreeable to the parties hereto. Such personnel and their salaries and expense allowances shall be subject to the approval of the Client.

Tests and Final Inspection

6. After the construction is completed, the Engineers shall perform such tests as are necessary to make certain that all equipment and construction fully complies with the plans and specifications. The Engineers shall make a final inspection of the work and shall certify its completion to the Client.

Plant Operations

7. The Engineers shall supervise initial operation of the [structure] and shall [e.g., instruct the Client's operating superintendent in the proper operation of the plant].

Records and Reports

8. The Engineers shall not be required, under the terms of this contract, to make property surveys necessary for acquisition of right-of-way or property. The Engineers shall, however, make all topographic and construction surveys.

Property Surveys

9. The Engineers shall not be required, under the terms of this contract, to make property surveys necessary for acquisition of right-of-way or property. The Engineers shall, however, make all topographic and construction surveys.

Time of Completion

10. The Engineers shall complete the plans and specifications within _____ days after date of execution of this contract.

Compensation

11. The Client shall compensate the Engineers for their services by the payment of the following fees:

   A. For surveys, preliminary plans and estimates, final plans and specifications, and general supervision of construction a percentage of construction costs in accordance with the following schedule:

The first $15,000 of construction cost	10 percent
Next $385,000 of construction cost	6 percent
Next $400,000 of construction cost	5½ percent
All over $800,000 of construction cost	5 percent

B. For resident supervison and inspection, a fee equal to [e.g., the salary paid the resident engineer and inspectors, plus 75 percent of such salary paid, and plus any expenses incurred by the resident engineer and inspectors in connection with the job and paid by the Engineers]. Construction cost is defined as the total cost of the project exclusive of the cost of engineering, legal service, land and right-of-way, and Client's overhead.

The fee shall be due and payable in the following manner:

The amount of _____ dollars ($_____) previously paid for the preliminary report will be considered as part payment of the fee stated above.

On completion of plans and specifications, their approval by the [e.g., State Department of Health] and presentation of plans and specifications, their approval by the [e.g., State Department of Health] and presentation of plans and specifications to the Client an amount equal to 70 percent of the computed fee in accordance with Schedule A above based on estimated construction cost and less amounts previously paid.

During the period of construction and proportionally with the progress of construction an amount equal to 20 percent of the fee in accordance with Schedule A above based on contract construction cost.

On completion of the project and final inspection, an amount equal to the total fee outlined above based on final construction cost, less amounts previously paid.

The fee for resident supervision and inspection as provided under Schedule B above will be billed and payable monthly.

Services Not Included

13. If, after the plans and specifications are completed and approved by the Client and [e.g., State Department of Health], the Engineers are required to change plans and specifications because of changes made by the Client, then the Engineers shall receive an additional fee for such changes that shall be based on their standard per diem fees.

Assistants

14. It is understood and agreed that the employment of the Engineers by the Client for the purpose aforesaid shall be exclusive, but the Engineers have the right to employ such assistants as they may deem proper in the performance of the work, said assistants to be employed subject to the approval of the Client, and the services of said assistants are to be paid for by the Engineers.

Assignment

15. This Agreement, and each and every portion thereof, shall be binding on the successors and assigns of the parties hereto, but the same shall not be assigned by the Engineers without written consent of the Client.

Executive, in duplicate, at [state], on the day and year first written above.

Client
[typed name of client]

By [signature]
(typed name and designation of person signing]

Engineers
[typed names of engineers]

By [signature]
[typed name and designation of person signing]

Sample of Agent Agreement

The following contract form is typical of the type of contract used when the consultant will act as an external agent for the client, usually with respect to selling or representing. This form of agreement is also typical of those used between a consultant and individuals retained by the consultant as subconsultants.

Consultant Agreement

This agreement made and entered into this _____ day of _____, 19XX, by and between _____ (hereinafter referred to as "Company") and _____ (hereinafter referred to as "Consultant") residing at _____.

In consideration of the mutual agreement herein contained, it is understood and agreed by and between the parties as follows:

I. Nature of Services
   A. Consultant is hereby authorized to procure clients for the Company. All funds received by the Consultant shall be received in trust for the Company and be delivered immediately to the Company. All checks or other negotiable instruments received by Consultant from client shall be made payable to the firm or firms designated from time to time by the Company.
   B. Consultant shall have the exclusive right to establish his own working hours and determine his own days of work.
   C. Consultant shall not be required to perform his services upon the Company's premises.
   D. Any business expenses incurred by Consultant, including but not limited to automobile, and the like, shall not be reimbursed by the Company.
   E. Consultant agrees to use his best efforts in conducting all of the activities referred to in this Agreement.
   F. Consultant agrees to refrain from taking any action to injure the Company or its reputation.
   G. Nothing contained herein shall be construed to create the relationship of Employer and Employee or Agent

and Principal between the Company and Consultant. Consultant shall conduct his business as an Independent Contractor and shall have no authority to create, alter, or amend any agreements or representations on behalf of the Company or to incur any liabilities for the Company. Consultant acknowledges that he is not an employee of the Company, and said Company is not obligated nor charged with the responsibility of withholding income taxes from any commissions due the Consultant nor is the Company obligated to pay Social Security taxes nor F.I.C.A. taxes upon or for the Consultant.

H. Consultant agrees to adhere to fair business principles and comply with all federal, state and local laws and regulations either existing or pending. Consultant further agrees to file applications for licensing, bonding, or other permits, and to pay all fees pertaining thereto as may be required by any regulatory body.

II. Solicitation and Termination

A. Consultant shall not make any misrepresentations or offer warranties or guarantees of any kind to its clients, the effect of which would be to induce the prospective clients to enter into an agreement with the Company. If a lawsuit should arise from misrepresentations made by the Consultant, the Consultant shall indemnify the Company for any and all damages incurred thereby, including court costs, legal fees and any judgments rendered or settlement costs incurred therefrom.

B. Consultant agrees that he will not issue, distribute, or circulate any advertising or promotional material, circulars, or pamphlets relating to the Company unless and until it has been authorized and approved in writing by the Company. The Consultant shall withdraw any said material and discontinue its use immediately upon the Company's written request to do so.

C. This Agreement may be terminated by either party upon giving written notice. Upon the giving of said notice, the Company shall cause to be paid to Consultant any monies due Consultant, as herein provided, and Consultant in turn shall reimburse the Company for any monies it advanced not earned, and return to the Company any material, products, stationery, samples, etc., which Consultant may have which belong to the Company. Upon termination of this Agreement for any reason, the Company shall have a secured lien over any accrued or accruing commissions due Consultant under the provisions of this Agreement or any amendment or addendum attached hereto, for monies owing from Consultant to Company, and for any damages sustained by the Company from conduct of the Consultant.

III. Compensation

In consideration of the functions performed hereunder by the Consultant, Company will pay Consultant $200 of the fees and/or deposits collected from bona fide clients acquired by the Consultant for the Company.

The above stated commission shall constitute the only source of compensation to the Consultant by the Company.

IV. Contract Enforcement

   A. This Agreement constitutes the entire agreement about understanding between the parties and supersedes any and all other agreements between the parties.

   B. No remedy granted to the Company by virtue of the Agreement shall be exclusive of any other legal or equitable remedy available to the Company existing by laws of statute.

V. Miscellaneous

   A. The parties agree and intend that all questions concerning this Agreement, including the validity, capacity of parties, effect interpretation and performance shall be governed by the laws of the State of _____.

B. The rights, privileges, duties, and obligations of both the Company and the Consultant to each other shall be limited to those specifically set forth herein.

C. This Agreement and the terms, conditions, and obligations herein contained shall be binding upon the parties hereto, their assigns, transferees, heirs, and legal representatives.

D. This Agreement shall not vest in Consultant, his heirs, estate, or legal representatives, any right, title, or interest in any assets in the Company itself, its name, good will, or other market business activities other than as set forth in this Agreement and only for so long as the Agreement has not been terminated, and not longer.

E. This Agreement constitutes the complete Agreement between the Consultant and the Company. No representation or promise, either oral or written, have been made except as specifically set forth herein. Should any part of this Agreement be declared invalid, such invalidity shall not affect the remainder of this Agreement. It is the intention of the parties that they would have executed the remaining portion of this Agreement without herein including any portion which may hereafter be declared invalid.

F. The forbearance or neglect by either party to insist upon the performance of this Agreement, or any part thereof, shall not constitute a waiver of any rights or privileges.

In Witness Whereof, the parties have executed this Agreement on the day and year first above written.

The foregoing is hereby agreed to:

_____

Consultant

[Company Name]

By _____

Sample Form of a Subconsulting Contract

The following form is included as an example of a contract a consultant might use in retaining the services of a second or subconsultant. The primary or master consultant is referred to as the "Company" and the assistant or subconsultant as "Consultant."

It will be obvious that this agreement form could be used by a client in retaining the services of a consultant, as well.

Consulting Agreement

The _____ was formed to serve the continuing and specialized education of technical and other professional groups and individuals. Through its unique programs of publishing seminars and workshop offerings, the _____ provides quality education tailored to the specialized needs of professionals in a real-world, performance-oriented environment. In the furtherance of this work, the president of the _____ (hereinafter called the President) desires to utilize the expert assistance of _____ (hereinafter called the Consultant) in the field or fields in which the Consultant has professional qualifications.

A.   Character and Extent of Services

1. It is the mutual intent of the parties that the Consultant shall act strictly in a professional consulting capacity as an independent contractor for all purposes and in all situations and shall not be considered an employee of the _____ (hereinafter called the Company).

2. The Consultant reserves full control of his activities as to the manner and selection of methods with respect to rendering his professional consulting services to the Company.

3. The Consultant agrees to perform his activities in accordance with the highest and best state of the art of his profession.

4. The Consultant is an independent contractor and shall provide worker's compensation insurance or self-insure his services. He shall also hold and keep blameless the

Company, its officers, agents, and employees thereof from all damages, costs, or expenses in law or equity that may at any time arise due to injury to, death of persons, or damage to property, including Company property, arising by reason of, or in the course of performance of this agreement; nor shall the Company be liable or responsible for any accident, loss, or damage, and the Consultant, at his own expense, cost, and risk, shall defend any and all actions, suits, or other legal proceedings that may be brought or instituted against the Company or officers or agents thereof on any claim or demand, and pay or satisfy any judgment that may be rendered against the Company or officers or agents thereof in any such action, suit, or legal proceeding.

B. Period of Service and Termination

1. The period of service by the Consultant under this agreement shall be from _____ through _____ and may be renewed upon the mutual agreement of the parties hereto.

2. Either the Company or the Consultant may terminate this agreement by giving the other party thirty days' written notice of intention of such action.

3. The President reserves the right to halt or terminate the conduct of a seminar/workshop by the Consultant without prior notice or claim for additional compensation should, in the opinion of the President, such conduct not be in the interests of the Company.

C. Compensation

1. Upon the Consultant's acceptance hereof, the Company agrees to pay the Consultant according to the following schedule: [insert compensation rate or fixed fee and any allowance for or schedule of allowable expenses, if any].

2. In the event that the Company desires, and it is mutually agreed to by the Consultant, the Consultant's services may be used in the conduct of seminars/

workshops not specifically identified in paragraph C.1. In such cases, the Company agrees to pay the Consultant on the basis of the following schedule:

[insert appropriate schedule]

3. In the event of special circumstances, variations to the fee schedule of paragraphs C.1 and C.2 will be allowed as mutually agreed to in writing by the parties hereto.

4. Notification: The Consultant will be notified by the President in writing to engage his participation in specific seminar(s) and/or workshop(s) to which the fee schedule of paragraphs C.1 and C.2 apply. Such notification will include a statement of the time(s) and place(s) of intended seminar/workshop conduct together with other information contributing to the successful conduct of the seminar/workshop sessions.

5. The Consultant, as an independent contractor, shall be responsible for any expenses incurred in the performance of this contract, except as otherwise agreed to in writing prior to such expenses being incurred. The Company will reimburse the Consultant for reasonable travel expenses incurred with respect thereto.

[a specification of "reasonable" may be inserted here]

D. Method of Payment

1. Having proper notification the Consultant shall be paid as provided for in paragraphs C.1 and C.2 hereof, on the basis of a properly executed "Claim for Consulting Service" form.

2. The "Claim for Consulting Service" form is to be submitted at the end of the calendar month during which consulting services are performed. Exception to this arrangement are allowed with the written approval of the President.

3. Payment to the Consultant will be made by check, delivered by certified mail postmarked no later than _____ days subsequent to receipt of the "Claim for Consulting Service" form as provided for in pargraphs D.1 and D.2.

E. Copyrights
1. The Consultant agrees that the Company shall determine the disposition of the title to and the rights under any copyright secured by the Consultant or his employee on copyrightable material first produced or composed and delivered to the Company under this agreement. The Consultant hereby grants to the Company a royalty-free, nonexclusive, irrevocable license to reproduce, translate, publish, use and dispose of, and to authorize others to do so, all copyrighted or copyrightable work not first produced or composed by the Consultant in the performance of this agreement but which is incorporated into the material furnished under this agreement, provided that such license shall be only to the extent the Consultant now has or, prior to the completion or final settlement of this agreement, may acquire the right to grant such license without becoming liable to pay compensation to others solely because of such grant.
2. The Consultant agrees that he will not knowingly include any copyrighted material in any written or copyrightable material furnished or delivered under this contract without a license as provided in paragraph E.1 hereof or without the consent of the author of the copyrighted material.
3. The Consultant agrees to report in writing to the Company promptly and in reasonable detail any notice or claim of copyright infringement received by the Consultant with respect to any material delivered under this agreement.

F. Drawings, Designs, Specifications

All drawings, sketches, designs, design data, specifications, notebooks, technical and scientific data, and all photographs, negatives, reports, findings, recommendations, data and memoranda of every description relating thereto, as well as all copies of the foregoing, relating to the work performed under this agreement or any part thereof, shall be subject to the inspection of the Company at all reasonable times; and the Consultant and his employees shall afford the Company proper facilities for such inspection; and further shall be the property of the Company and may be used by the Company for any purpose whatsoever without any claim on the part of the Consultant and his employees for additional compensation, and subject to the right of the Consultant to retain a copy of said material shall be delivered to the Company or otherwise disposed of by the Consultant, either as the Company may from time to time direct during the progress of the work, or in any event, as the Company shall direct upon the completion or termination of this agreement.

G. Assignment

The Company reserves the right to assign all or any part of its interest in and to this assignment. The Consultant may not assign or transfer this agreement, any interest therein or claim thereunder without the written approval of the Company.

In Witness Whereof, the parties have executed this agreement.

Consultant   _____
                                                            Company

_____   _____

Date _____   Date _____

Sample of a Fixed Price Service Contract

The following agreement serves as an example of a consultant providing a specific set of services within a definite time period for a fixed dollar sum. In this example, the consultant is referred to as the "Contractor" and the client, an institution of higher education, as the "University."

Agreement

This Agreement is made, this _____ day of _____, 19XX, by and between _____, hereinafter referred to as the "University," and "Contractor."

Witnesseth

Whereas, the University desires to develop and conduct a training program for its personnel and the personnel of such other eligible education agencies as may become participants in this program; and

Whereas, the purposes of said training program are to:

> Upgrade the managerial and technical skills of career counseling and placement personnel; and increase the professional stature of career counseling and placement personel; and provide a cadre of trained professionals appropriate materials to continue further training as required with minimum funding support needed; and provide a vehicle for the ongoing assessment of in-service training needs of career counseling and placement personnel; and

Whereas, the Contractor is particularly skilled and competent to conduct such a management training program; and

Whereas, funds for this contract are budgeted for and included in a federal project plan approved under _____, and as described in the program prospectus identified as Grant _____, which is hereinafter referred to as the "Project;" and

Whereas, said Project was approved [date] and project expenditures approved on [date]

Now, therefore, it is mutually agreed as follows:

1. The term of this Agreement shall be for the period commencing [date], continuing to and until [date].

2. The Contractor agrees to develop and conduct a training program consisting in part of a series of three workshop session presentations. Each of said workshop presentations shall be of eight hours' duration and shall be conducted at [place]. The aforesaid training program shall be developed and conducted by the Contractor in accordance with the project prospectus submitted by the University for funding under _____ and in particular with the "attachment" to said program prospectus, which is marked Exhibit "A," attached hereto and by reference incorporated herein.

3. The aforesaid workshop presentations shall include three days of intensive training using an approach that has demonstrated considerable success working with career counseling and placement personnel of this type. Specific workshop topic coverage shall include the following:

[insert information]

4. The training workshop will be conducted during the contract term in accordance with a schedule mutually agreed upon by the University and the Contractor.

5. In connection with the conducting and development of the training program, the Contractor agrees as follows:

   a. The Contractor will plan for and prepare such materials as are needed to conduct the various program sessions as described. Such material preparation and development will include the preparation of participant resource material, development of worksheets, orientation materials, participant guides, and handbooks. All materials developed will reflect the highest standards of quality applicable to educational material development.

   b. The Contractor will provide expert session facilitation staff as follows:

   A minimum of one (1) expert staff for the first twelve (12) participants in attendance at each session; further the Contractor will provide one (a) additional expert staff for each additional twelve (12) participants in attendance at each session to a maximum of forty-eight total participants per session.

   c. The Contractor will regularly consult with designated personnel of the University to monitor program progress and planned activities so as to improve and strengthen the overall program.

6. The Contractor further agrees to:

   a. Furnish the University on or before [date] with a final report. This report will describe all relevant aspects of program activity and will be in such style and format as to comply with the requirements of the enabling grant.

   b. Prepare appropriate presession and postsession participant testing materials to enable the ongoing assessment of the overall program activities. The Contractor shall collect, analyze, and interpret these findings as an integral part of the program development and conduct activity.

   c. Conduct, within four to six months after the conclusion of the workshop presentations, a posttest follow-up survey that will seek to discover what difficulties, if any, the participants in the program have encountered in applying the principles developed in the workshop training activity to career counseling and placement problems. A component of the follow-up survey will probe for participant attitude and individual assessment of the relevancy of the workshop training activity and the topic material in the context of program administration experience during the intervening period.

   d. Furnish the University with copies of all written and visual materials produced for distribution to workshop participants. The Contractor will retain no proprietary rights to such materials, said rights being vested to the University.

7. The University agrees as follows:

   a. To designate one of its staff members as Project Director to represent the University in all technical matters pertaining to this program.

   b. To arrange the necessary preprogram advertisement

and participant notification so as to encourage participation.

c. To provide or otherwise arrange for facilities that are adequate to conduct the workshop sessions.

d. To limit session attendance, exclusive of Contractor staff, to the maximum eligible number of participants _____ plus up to three (3) additional nonparticipating persons.

e. To make necessary arrangements with participating educational agencies to make personnel available as participants in all specified training activities.

f. To arrange for use on an as-available basis of University instructional equipment, including 16mm sound projectors, overhead transparency projectors, 35mm slide projectors, tape recorders, and/or related audio visual equipment, as requested by the Contractor in response to program requirements. The University agrees to provide competent personnel to operate all such equipment. The University will provide adequate maintenance and care of such equipment and will provide operational assistance to the Contractor as requested.

g. To distribute to program participants at the request of the Contractor, various project materials relevant to the program. Such materials may include training session handout material, descriptive information, questionnaires, and announcements.

h. To provide or arrange for assistance to the Contractor at training session locations as mutually agreed in connection with facility arrangements, scheduling, and other matters pertaining to the successful conduct of the program.

8. It is expressly understood and agreed by both parties hereto that the Contractor, while engaging in carrying out and complying with any of the terms and conditions of this contract, is an independent Contractor and is not an officer, agent, or employee of the University.

9. The Contractor shall provide worker's compensation insurance or self-insure his services. He shall also hold and keep harmless the University and all officers, agents, and employees thereof from all damages, costs of expenses in law or equity that may at any time arise or be set up because of injury to or death of persons or damage to property, including University property, arising by reason of, or in the course of the performance of this contract; nor shall the University be liable or responsible for any accident, loss, or damage, and the Contractor, at his own expense, cost, and risk, shall defend any and all actions, suits, or other legal proceedings that may be brought or instituted against the University or officers or agents thereof on any claim or demand, and pay or satisfy any judgment that may be rendered against the University or officers or agents thereof in any such action, suit, or legal proceeding.

10. In consideration of the satisfactory performance of the Contractor, the University agrees to reimburse the Contractor in the amount of Fifteen Thousand Dollars ($15,000) in accordance with the following schedule:

30 May 19XX	$ 4,000
30 June 19XX	$ 5,000
30 July 19XX	$ 4,000
30 August 19XX	$ 2,000
	$15,000

In witness whereof, each party has caused this agreement to be executed by its duly authorized representative on the date first mentioned above.

Contractor   University

_____   _____
Name   Name
Title   Title

Sample Professional Services Agreement

This Agreement is made this _____ day of _____, 19XX, between _____, hereinafter the Company, doing business at _____, and _____, hereinafter referred to as Consultant, doing business at _____.

1. Statement of Work: During the terms of this Agreement, Consultant will perform services as requested from time to time by the Company, at such place or places and at such times as shall be mutually agreeable to the parties hereto. The services shall relate to preparing contract or sub-contract draft documents for review by Company attorney or conducting seminars as agreed by the parties.

2. Payment: The Company shall pay Consultant according to the following schedule:

   a. Hourly fee of $_____ or flat fee as agreed to in writing by the parties.

   b. Travel Expense: The Company shall reimburse Consultant for the actual cost of transportation (except for normal commuting), lodging and subsistence as authorized by _____. Travel expenses will be paid only in accordance with the effective policy of the Company covering such expenses.

   c. Other Expenses: The Company shall reimburse Consultant for all other reasonable actual expenses incidental to the services performed here under which have been approved in advance by _____.

   d. Invoices: Payment for compensation and reimbursement for expenses incurred will be made thirty days after submission by the Consultant of invoice. The invoices should be submitted at least monthly and should specify the period for which compensation is claimed; and travel costs and other expenses claimed must be itemized. The invoices must be substantiated by receipts for transportation and lodging and all other items of expenses amounting to more than $10 where receipts are normally issued.

The invoices should be submitted to _____.

e. Total costs under this Agreement may not exceed $_____ unless approved in advance by the Company in writing.

3. Other obligations: The Consultant represents and warrants to the Company that he is now under no contract or agreement, nor has he previously executed any documents whatsoever with any other person, firm, association, or corporation that will, in any manner, prevent his giving, and the Company from receiving, the benefit of his services and related inventions or contrivances that may be devised by him, or developed under his direction, in accordance with the terms of the Agreement. The Company agrees that, during the term of this Agreement or any extension or renewal thereof, the Consultant may be employed by other persons, firms, or corporations engaged in the same or similar business as that of the Company, provided, however, that the provisions of Section 5 hereof shall be strictly observed by the Consultant with respect to such other persons, firms, or corporations.

4. Termination: This Agreement commences on the date written above and shall terminate on [date]. By mutual consent, the Agreement may be extended for an additional period or periods of _____. Either party may terminate this Agreement at any time by giving written notice to the other party.

5. Patents and Data:

a. Title: Consultant agrees that the Company shall have sole ownership and title to all rights and legal interest in:
   (1) All data, drawings, designs, analyses, graphs, reports, products, tooling, physical property, and all other items or concepts, computer programs, and
   (2) All inventions, discoveries, and improvements, whether patentable or not, conceived or reduced

to practice during the terms of this Agreement, relating to subject matter prepared, procured, produced, or worked on by Consultant, his associates or employees, arising out of or relating to the service or work performed hereunder.

b. Disclosures and Assignments: Consultant agrees to make full disclosure to the Company of all items included in section 5a above and, to the extent that Consultant may be so requested by the Company, Consultant agrees to execute and deliver to the Company assignments, in forms satisfactory to the Company of such items. Consultant also agrees to do or perform, or cause to be done or performed, with the Company bearing all legal and all out-of-pocket expenses, therefore, all lawful acts deemed by the Company to be necessary for the preparation and prosecution of applications for and the procurement, issuance, maintenance, enforcement, and defense of patents and/or copyrights, throughout the world, based on inventions and/or subject matter included in section 5a above. The Company will bear all expenses incurred in the enforcement and defense of all such patents and/or copyrights.

c. Information made available to Consultant or which Consultant becomes privy to, or produced by or for him pursuant to this Agreement, during the term of this Agreement, shall be considered proprietary information supplied in confidence, and shall not be disclosed to others, or used for manufacture or any other purposes except as required under this Agreement, without prior written permission by the Company.

d. Nothing herein shall be construed as an implied patent license under any patents of the Company.

e. Consultant agrees to obtain an agreement similar to this section 5 from any agent, employee, or associate of this Agreement.

6. Security: Consultant will comply with all applicable security regulations of the United States Government and of the Company.

7. Government Contract Requirements: This Agreement is/ is not issued pursuant to Government contract _____. If this Agreement is for an amount in excess of $2,500 and a government contract number or the word "Classified" is stated, the following is applicable:

    a. Audit and Records: Consultant agrees that his books, records, and such of his facilities as may be engaged in the performance of this order shall at all reasonable times be subject to inspection and audit by the government department having jurisdiction of the prime contract noted. The controller general of the United States or any of his duly authorized representatives shall, until the expiration of three years after final payment under this Agreement, have access to and the right to examine any directly pertinent books, documents, papers, and records of Consultant involving transactions related to this Agreement.

    b. Security: In the event this order requires access to any classified information or material classified as "Confidential" or higher, the provision of DAR clause 7-104.12 shall be applicable. The Company reserves the right, and Consultant agrees to such reservation, to terminate this Agreement at any time if the Consultant is not at all times authorized to handle such classified matter by the appropriate government agency.

8. Subcontracting: Consultant will not subcontract or assign any of the work or rights hereunder without prior written approval of the Company.

9. Relationship of Consultant: Consultant will serve as independent contractor, and this Agreement will not be deemed to create a partnership, joint enterprise, or employment between the parties. Consultant is required to make

appropriate filings with the taxing authorities as a self-employed person to account for and make all payments required by the local, state and federal taxing authorities to include income tax, social security, and SDI payments, and Consultant further agrees to indemnify and hold the Company harmless for any claims made by the above-mentioned taxing authorities resulting from performance made by Consultant in performance of this Agreement. If the Company determines that taxes should be withheld, the Company reserves the right to unilaterally withhold as appropriate and notify the Consultant accordingly.

10. Interpretation of contract: This Agreement may not be changed except in writing, signed by Consultant and authorized procurement official of the Company. This writing contains the entire agreement between the parties. The validity, performance, construction, and effect of this Agreement shall be governed by the laws of the state or commonwealth in which the Company has an address and place of business as set forth in the first paragraph of this Agreement.

In Witness Whereof, the parties hereto have executed this Agreement as of the day and year first above written.

The Company

By: _____

Title: _____

The Consultant

Engagement Letter

There are certain situations in which an engagement is of such limited duration and/or where the time between scheduling an appointment and providing the consulting service is so short that entering into a contract between the parties is impractical. Yet the consultant may still desire to inform the client of the terms and conditions under which he is willing to provide services. In such cases, an engagement letter may be used.

It is a good idea to provide your client with a letter that acknowledges the engagement you and the client have agreed upon. There are several features such a letter should contain:

1. Acknowledge the time and place where the first formal/ work meeting will take place.

2. Specify the purpose of the first meeting and the purpose of the consultation in general.

3. Indicate the time or duration you expect will be involved in the consultation, or a statement as to why it is not possible to provide such an estimate.

4. Communicate what the fee will be for the services to be provided, if possible, or indicate the basis on which the fee will be charged.

5. Specify the payment arrangements as well as the invoice schedule. In the past, consultants have generally been satisfied with telling clients when the invoice will be sent, leaving "trade custom" to govern when payments will be made. With trade custom increasingly turning into sixty to ninety days or more, it is a good idea to inform the client, and obtain his approval, for a more reasonable period of time between invoice date and payment date.

Sample Engagement Letter
[letterhead]

Date

John Q. Doe, President
Doe Industries
1234 Main Street
Anytown, Anystate Zip

Dear Mr. Doe:

This letter will confirm our telephone conversation of this morning. It is my understanding that we will meet for a full day May 19 at your office to develop a proposal for the sale of your Widgets to XYZ industries. I will arrive at 8:30 a.m.

Please be advised that the fee for my services is [amount] a day. It is my policy to work on an advance retainer basis. Under such an arrangement, my clients deposit with me any sum they wish and I invoice against the retainer which has been deposited. Funds deposited but not used are returned.

Because of the short time between now and our meeting, you may either forward your check for [amount] in advance of our meeting or plan to pay for services at the consultation.

I look forward to working with you next week on what should be a most interesting project.

Sincerely,

Consultant

Summary

Working under some form of written agreement is necessary in the consulting business; even if no difficulties or disagreements ever occur between client and consultant, a written contract improves the quality of communications between the parties concerned.

In particular, a written agreement provides for:

1. Avoidance of misunderstanding

2. Assurance of performance and results—for the client to have this assurance, the contract should provide the following:
   A. Time schedule
   B. Requirement for insurance coverage.
   C. Provision preventing subcontracting or assignment of the contract to someone else by one party without the written consent of the other party.
   D. Provisions (and penalties) for termination of the consultation.
   E. If desired, request for the assignment of specific people to perform the services.
   F. Other provisions such as requirements that the consultant obtain any necessary government approvals, maintain adequate records, make periodic reports to the client, and so forth.

Components of the contract:

   I. Preamble section
  II. Project approaches
 III. Consultant's tasks
 IV. Company's tasks
  V. Special conditions
 VI. Payment of consulting fees
VII. Option to amend the contract

12
How Clients Get
Free Consulting

There are some clever ways that knowing clients have adopted to obtain free consulting from overly helpful and undisciplined consultants.

Proposal Writing

If the consultant writes a recipe rather than a proposal, you may not need to pay for the consultant's services. Often, by requesting greater detail and specificity, the client can cause an inalert consultant to produce detailed documentation on exactly how the consultation will be conducted. Once in hand, the client may discover that the need for a consultant has greatly diminished.

This is particularly a problem for technical consultants, who, while having written many proposals, may lack experience in writing consulting proposals. They tend to turn out voluminous documents outlining detailed procedures that internal staff can adopt and put into action. Every step is spelled out, every activity, every time sequence. So the client decides the consultant's services are not needed and then has an internal staff member implement the proposal. Thus, experienced consultants may be very cautious about putting too many substantive details about implementation into proposals because they do not want the client to be able to make the necessary changes or perform the necessary activities without the consultants' services.

Follow-Up

After the consulting assignment is complete, the client might call the consultant on the telephone and say, "We don't understand this. It isn't working here. Could you stop by tomorrow and help us with this, that, etc.?" Such requests may be legitimate. In the interest of being helpful, professional, and comprehensive, however, consultants frequently provide more detailed or long-lasting assistance than is really necessary or appropriate under the terms of the initial client-consultant agreement. A shrewd client knows this and turns it to his or her advantage.

Diagnosis/Needs Analysis

The client might continue to have the consultant provide free diagnostic or needs analysis services on the presumption that if the diagnosis shows there is a problem, the consultant will be given a contract. About 85 percent of the time, after the problem is identified and explained to the client—which may be the most beneficial aspect of the consultation—the client sees no reason to take action, at least with respect to involving or requiring the services of the consultant. In short, the client has obtained a no-charge diagnostic study.

Future Riches

Clients have been known to promise "future riches." Clients say they cannot afford to pay the consultant now and then entice him or her with promises of exposure to important or influential people, unique opportunities and experiences, and promises of big business later on in the future. Some, not all, consultants will fall prey to such logic. There is something almost seductive about the promise of future riches from a major client: "Do you know what an opportunity it is to work with a company like ours? Do you know what that is going to do for your consulting practice? Do you realize the people you are going to meet?" Many consultants cave in and say they will not charge the client this time or will charge less than they usually do. Knowing that some consultants will acquiesce to obtain professional and/or client exposure for future consulting opportunities, creative clients thus obtain the services of such professionals at substantial savings.

Diversion

A consultant's professional nature makes him or her want to do a complete, accurate, and professional job. For the most part, the very nature of the consultant's personality is helpfulness. He or she wants to see things done properly, effectively, and completely. A client who knows this can get a consultant to handle small, add-on, related projects "at no additional charge."

If your consultant is working on a daily or hourly rate, there will be no diversion. The consultant will simply charge for the additional days or hours expended. On a fixed-price or fixed-fee basis, however, the client can get a great deal more per dollar expended than he or she perhaps ever imagined.

While you, the client, do want to get the most out of your consultant's services, you will probably achieve a better client-consultant relationship and more valuable services and results from the consultation if you are honest and straightforward with the consultant. The consultant knows you want your money to be well spent and the consultation to be well worth your money; however, if the consultant feels you are being less than honest, or less than equitable, he or she will probably treat you accordingly—finishing the job and fulfilling your needs adequately, but probably no more than that.

13
How Consultants Say No
or Get Their Own Way

C onsultants do not always say yes. Consultants do not always
want to work with you. When they elect not to handle your
assignment, they likely do not just say, "No, thank you." They
have certain turndown phrases, each with its own meaning.

"I Don't Do That."

When a consultant says he or she would like to work with you
but does not do your sort of job or project, the consultant is most
often really saying that he or she does not want to get involved
with you at all but does not want to just say no to you.

"I'm Too Busy."

When a consultant says he or she would like to help you but is
just too busy right now, the consultant is really saying that he or
she does not want to work with you. Now you might ask yourself why. Is it the money? Is it the job? Is it the personality? Did
you ask the consultant to do things that were illegal, unethical,
unprofessional, or just undesirable? Is there a conflict of interest?
There are reasons why a consultant will not get involved, and it
may sometimes (not always) be worth your effort to figure out
why a consultant does not want to become involved with you and
your project.

Redefinition

When the consultant takes your job, turns it around, redefines it, and does it on his or her own terms, the consultant is saying that he or she did not want to work with you the way you wanted to work but does want to work with you on his or her own terms. You must be careful, however, that when the consultant turns the job around and redefines it the consultant has not increased your cost or decreased the probability of success in the accomplishments you seek. It is permissible for consultants to redefine the job. If they have done similar projects, they probably have, in many cases, better ways of fulfilling your needs and doing the job than might have initially occurred to you. But you need to be alert and aware and make sure that in redefining, the consultant does not change your objectives, does not change your purposes.

Often the consultant is acting in the client's best interest by redefining the project or reassessing the problem, although the client may not realize or may not want to realize that the redefinition is in his or her best interest.

Consider an example. An orthodontist is having difficulties with practice management. Specifically, she is not realizing the income she should even though her productivity is excellent. She calls in a consultant, telling him to identify and resolve the problem but stipulates that the consultant need not investigate personnel management; the orthodontist has that area under control and the consultant need not worry about it.

Across the street, an independent hardware dealer is losing business to a large chain store because, as he tells the consultant, his inventory always seems to be down and he is often out of stock on many popular items. He is sure his system is fine, though; he just wants the consultant to figure out a way for the merchandise to be shipped to him more expeditiously or figure out a formula to measure turnaround time.

Both the orthodontist and the hardware dealer want the consultant's help—they want the consultant to solve their problems; however, they do not want the consultant to reassess or redefine their problems. Perhaps personnel management is fine in the dental practice, and maybe the inventory control system in the hardware store is satisfactory. But perhaps not. Those areas may be the very ones the consultant needs to assess and improve upon to solve his clients' problems. If such is the case, the consultant can either go directly to his clients and say that the problems need to be redefined so that he can solve them, or he can go along with the clients' wishes but pay special but subtle attention to those off-limit areas.

Since the consultant is familiar with dental practices, he knows that virtually everything revolves around the staff—appointment control, bookkeeping, collection procedures. So it is a good possibility that the one area that is off limits is also the one most in need of scrutiny. But perhaps the orthodontist is particularly proud of her relationship with her staff and does not want an expert telling her that she has not taken care of all that she should or that she needs to improve her management abilities in some areas. Or perhaps she is afraid that although she and her employees get along well, she is not managing them adequately. Therefore, she establishes an out-of-bounds area. Once the consultant senses that the orthodontist is sensitive about her management ability, how does he promote change? Carefully.

The consultant subtly redefines the problem when suggesting a solution to the orthodontist. He suggests to the client that cash flow problems can be taken care of by placing more emphasis on collection activity, both at the time of service and on the phone. Since collection chores are not the favorite of employees, step-by-step procedures, requiring close supervision in this area, can be spelled out by the consultant. The consultant tactfully suggests that since the orthodontist's time is best spent with patients, the consultant can set up the procedures and provide training and supervision for the staff. Also, the consultant can provide an employee assessment to be used in regular performance evaluations of the new procedures. The consultant leaves the client an out—without realizing that the consultant is well-informed about the off-limits area, the client can decide to involve herself more in personnel management, implementing the consultant's suggestions, or can assign that task to the consultant on a contract basis. The consultant has not assaulted the client's pride, and the orthodontist now has a chance to improve her management abilities with help from the consultant and thus improve her practice. Using such an approach, the consultant can deal with the entire scope of the problem, including personnel management.

Across the street at the hardware store, the consultant addresses the retailer's problems. From a stock employee, the consultant learns how ineffective the inventory control system really is. The boss does not want to change because he knows nothing about computers and does not want to lose control of his store to a machine. The consultant assesses this information and incorporates it into a problem in Receiving which gives him the opportunity to suggest a computer system for better inventory control. The consultant tells the client that the receiving department—and so far only the receiving department—needs streamlining. Too much merchandise sits on the dock after delivery and it is not being quickly broken down, inventoried, and displayed. He suggests to the retailer that a computer program could be used to speed up transfer of goods to the shelves. This recommendation in itself does not address the heart of the inventory problem because it only pertains to logging in of merchandise, but it allows the client to become familiar with the benefits of a computer without directly threatening his system or his sense of control. However, once the retailer sees that the computer is controllable in this one aspect of his business and sees what a benefit it can be to the store, his defenses may begin to drop. The consultant allows the client to feel his way around this new area of computer products and is able to guide him to his own eventual realization that the hardware store's whole inventory control system can and should be updated along with receiving, ordering, and billing. The consultant has gradually redefined the client's problem and possible solution by allowing the hardware retailer to slowly come to the same realization himself—that the old inventory control system is outdated and that a new a computerized inventory control system is necessary.

These two examples are ways the consultant can accept an assignment while redefining it. In these cases, the redefinition is subtle—the consultant never actually tells the client he is redefining the problems. By reading between the lines and anticipating the client's real needs, and by being subtle and tactful in actions and suggestions, the consultant was able to fulfill the client's needs and forestall the disappointment and possible hostility that rapid-fire recommendations and redefinition might have caused.

So, a consultant may redefine your problem—or the cause of your problem—without your awareness. Or he or she may come right out and say your problem needs redefining. However, it is probably in your best interest not to set off-limit areas (unless absolutely necessary—for example, regarding proprietary information) and to be completely candid with your consultant. In return, the consultant should be open and honest with you, facilitating an open consulting relationship and successful results.

High Bid

Some consultants will intentionally high-bid a job just to avoid having to do it. You come to the consultant with a job, asking him or her to bid on it, and the reluctant and unwilling consultant who does not want to work for you gives an overly high bid. If it is a $3,000 job, the consultant bids it at $6,000 and figures that if he or she gets it, it will not be as bad as it was at $3,000. So you need to be careful when the bid seems unusually high; it may be an indication that the consultant does not want to work with you.

Conflict of Interest

Three words a consultant can say to a client that will send the client running in the other direction are "conflict of interest." Whether there exists a conflict of interest is not the issue here. The fact is if there is a conflict of interest, you are already afraid you have said too much. You do not want to talk any more; you want everything you said to be forgotten. And so you, the client, go running in the opposite direction, which may be precisely what the consultant wanted. A conflict of interest for the consultant: "I'm sorry I can't design your cars, Mr. Ford. I already designed General Motors."

A Piece of the Assignment

Finally, sometimes consultants want to take just part of the job. You offer the consultant a great big assignment, and the consultant says he or she does not want it because it is not the consultant's area of specialty. The consultant agrees to do a very specific, small part of it if you will get someone else to do the rest.

Now you have to decide, do you want to manage more than one consultant? Do you want to manage five or six people to do the whole job? Many times the client will decide he or she does not want to manage that many people and would rather hand over the entire job to one consultant. In that case, this consultant who only wants to do a small part of the assignment is not the right consultant for you. Or perhaps you will let this consultant do a portion of the job for you but hold him or her responsible for coming up with other consultants to do the rest of the work and for managing their particular tasks and activities.

Summary

Six ways in which consultants refuse a job or turn a consulting job around to their advantage are:

1. "I Don't Do That"—The consultant says he or she would like to work with you but does not do your sort of job or project.
2. "I'm Too Busy"—The consultant says he or she would like to work with you but just does not have the time.
3. Redefinition—The consultant does want to work with you, but only on his or her terms, so the consultant takes the job, turning it around and redefining it.
4. High Bid—The consultant does not want to work with you but decides the job will be worth the money if you accept his or her overly high bid.
5. Conflict of Interest—If the consultant does not want to work with you, all he or she has to say is that there is a conflict of interest and generally that will send you running.

6. A Piece of the Assignment—The consultant does want to work with you but only wants to handle part of the project; he or she offers to do part of the job, leaving you to find someone else for the rest of it.

Sometimes consultants have very real, recognizable reasons for refusing to work with you, perhaps there really is a conflict of interest, of operating styles, or of personalities. But if the reasons are less clear, you might do well to consider why a consultant does not want to work with you—analyze your needs, your project, your personality, the price you are willing to pay, etc. By understanding why a consultant would not want to work for you, you may discover why a consultant *would* want to work for you and, thus, find the perfect consultant for your job.

14
Making the Client-Consultant Relationship Function Smoothly
Managing Consultants Effectively

P resumably, you have by now successfully overcome the trials of selecting a consultant, understanding the consulting process and the consultant's fees, and drafting some type of contract. You are now ready to let your chosen consultant go to work and bring you your desired results. However, you, the client, need to be prepared to contribute to the consulting relationship to make it function smoothly and successfully.

Consultants are expensive and will not do a good job for you unless you give them very clear directions or the responsibility for finding the directions. Be willing to pay for what their services are worth. Do not nickel and dime on small considerations. If your resources are limited then scale down the scope of work on this particular project. Consultants charge what they think they have to charge to stay in business. Sometimes they make too little money and sometimes they make too much, because of their inability to always estimate correctly. Neither client nor consultant likes to feel taken advantage of, so set measurable objectives and completion dates. Think through your problems beforehand.

Prepare your organization for the arrival of the consultant. Ensure that your employees do not see him or her as a threat to their own job security. A consultant needs to be properly introduced and supported, and, ideally, needs to have someone in the organization run interference for him or her to be most effective.

Work only with a written agreement. It does not have to be a formal contract that takes a battery of lawyers to understand, but it should be a specific agreement that spells out each party's obligation and responsibility.

Once you have made these provisions to enhance your use of the consultant, your job is not yet over—it is never really over, for you still need to manage your consultant. One of the primary reasons that consultants fail is lack of proper management on the part of the client. I did not say supervision; it is not the client's responsibility to supervise the consultant. The consultant is an independent contractor, a self-motivated, self-starting individual. But it is your responsibility to manage. You cannot abdicate management of the consultant if he or she is to satisfactorily serve your needs and accomplish the project at hand. To successfully manage a consultant, you should keep in mind several facts and factors, and if I sound like a broken record as I reiterate things I have said in previous chapters, it is because these notions are paramount in achieving a good client-consultant relationship and solving your problem or meeting your project goals.

Precise Objectives

To get good results from a consultant, you need to set precise objectives for the consultant's performance—as precise as possible. The consultant needs to know clearly exactly what he or she is expected to do and when he or she is expected to do it.

Observable Milestones

When at all possible, you want to establish observable milestones, perhaps in weekly intervals, biweekly intervals, or monthly intervals, and you want to take time to make sure the milestones have been reached. If there is any lack of quality or performance at the milestone points, this needs to be communicated to the consultant and the appropriate changes or corrections made.

Written Contract

You want to work with some form of written contract as an agreement. A written—as opposed to verbal—contract or agreement, in my experience, is absolutely vital for a successful consultant-client relationship. The reason is not that each party is going to sue the other; consultants and clients rarely go to court. Rather, the reason is that it clarifies communication. Verbal communications are sloppy. Proposals are inaccurate and do not communicate actual needs and objectives very well. But a written agreement outlining each party's responsibilities, obligations, and duties, will in fact, identify certain potential problems or failures that could occur in the consultation. Whenever possible, get these decided upon and corrected before the consultation begins.

There are, of course, consultants and clients who do not work on written contracts, but they often regret it later. A job worth doing is worth doing right and professionally. It may take longer to have a written contract or agreement—someone has to write it, people have to read it, lawyers may be involved in the writing or approving—but you will probably end up with a better project result.

Progress Reports

An interim or progress report is any report delivered to the client before the final report. Usually it is given at regular intervals, such as once a month in a long consultation. A progress report is usually given when specific milestones are reached. As the client, you should insist on progress reports, and you should perhaps, if your consultant does not, outline what should be in that progress report. An adequate progress report normally consists of the following:

1. Activities accomplished since the last progress report.

2. Planned activities that will be undertaken or accomplished between now and the next progress report.

3. Problems encountered in accomplishing these activities.

4. Problems anticipated in the next reporting period.

5. Suggestions for the client as to what the client could be doing to speed along, improve, or otherwise help the consultant's services.

As a client, you can easily become worried about the progress the consultant is making on a long assignment. Interim and progress reports reassure the client that the consultant is delivering high-quality service, and improve the quality of communication. From the client's point of view, the interim report serves as a checkup that enables the consultant to make necessary adjustments if the project is not proceeding as planned. It increases the chances that the consultation will be successful and the client satisfied. And it documents the progress that has been made and improves planning and scheduling.

Progress reports can be long, narrative documents containing visual or graphic material, data, memos, and letters, or they can be short reports. The longer, fully documented reports are generally required of government contracts. Long reports are also appropriate when large capital expenditures are involved. However, in most cases, short reports of about three to five pages are used. The progress or interim report should be tailored to the individual consultation; thus, if you decide to use progress reports, you and the consultant can agree on the appropriate length and content.

There are several important benefits to the progress report:

1. The client is ensured of being kept informed of progress, especially if personal contact between client and consultant is limited, as is sometimes the case.

2. The client gains a specific sense of control over the project by being able to oversee the work and its progress.

3. The client or decision maker has better information when reporting to superiors.

4. Regular communication increases client involvement, better ensuring client satisfaction.

5. In the event a dispute arises, reports provide written proof of what has been said and done.

6. Writing interim reports forces the consultant to discipline himself or herself throughout the project and to adhere to the time schedule.

7. Interim reports can act as procedural guides and continuing references throughout the project.

8. Interim reports can target problems that might impede the progress and success of the project.

A report should be clear, concise, well-written, and professional; it should be relevant to the project and should always address the project's goals and objectives. The progress report should also:

1. Estimate the percentage of the project completed by measuring work accomplished rather than proportion of time or money expended—unless the project is going over budget or over time, an issue that should certainly be addressed.

2. Emphasize results. The progress report should not place importance on events that do not represent or contribute to progress—unless the events pose problems for the project that need to be examined.

3. Avoid jargon and codes that do not communicate effectively and may be a substitute for lack of results.

4. Use graphs, charts, and other visual aids when appropriate to help present material and convey information.

5. Report only facts and data based on demonstrable facts. The consultant should avoid unsupported claims: he or she should also avoid hyperbole and superlatives—the progress should speak for itself.

6. Be as brief and concise as possible—long enough to communicate what needs to be communicated but short enough to avoid boring or confusing the reader.

7. Be made on time. The consultant should meet the deadlines the client and consultant establish. The progress report should be written as scheduled, even if the actual progress is behind schedule.

You may want to keep some of these factors in mind when reviewing a consultant's progress report.

The progress report is a way of promoting client-consultant communication, and you should use it as such. Once the consultant gives the client the report, it is the client's responsibility to take whatever action is needed. Perhaps the report indicates that the consultant needs additional time, personnel, or cooperation; you need to address these needs. Perhaps you feel that progress is not going as well as anticipated; it is your responsibility to speak with the consultant and discuss possible problems. Or perhaps the progress report suggests that progress is well under way and the project is going well; your mind is put to ease and, reassured that you know what is going on and do have control of the project, you can let the consultant do his or her work.

Even though these types of communication should be going on verbally every day, it is still useful once or twice a month to document progress in writing. The written word has a greater impact on most people's behavior than the verbal. People get busy, and people forget. However, if it is in writing, if it is a formal report, if it is in the files, it is going to cause everyone to pay more attention and to take action if any is indicated.

The following is an example of a written progress report, written in memo form.

[Letterhead]

MEMORANDUM

TO: (Name of Client)
               (Title or Position)
               (Organization)

FROM: (Name of Consultant)

DATE: (Date of Report)

SUBJECT: Progress Report Number 2
               Effective Time Management Training Program

This is the second of three reports to advise you on the status of the design and implementation of the Effective Time Management training program.

As of the date of the first interim report, _____, we had completed interviewing the sample of training program participants. Based upon their feedback, and upon the information you provided me, the following program outline and objectives were determined:

Training program outline:

1. Introduction—identifying the most important time management challenge.

2. Goal-Setting

3. Individual Traits Affecting Time Management

4. Job and Company Traits Affecting Time Management

5. Overcoming Common Challenges in Time Management

6. Review of Time Management Techniques

7. Developing a Personal Time Management Program

8. Motivation, Procrastination, and Commitment

Training program objectives:

1. Identify most important time management challenge.

2. Set meaningful and effective goals for on-the-job objectives.

3. Identify individual traits affecting time management, and select the right techniques to suit these traits.

4. Identify the job and company traits affecting time management and select the right techniques to suit these traits.

5. Identify personal habit patterns that interfere with effective time management and construct a plan to change them.

6. Construct a personal program for time management, based upon individual traits, job and company traits, and personal habit patterns.

It was also determined that an attitude measure on the various aspects of effective time management, employing Likert scales numbered 1 to 7 for each item, would be used as a pretraining and posttraining measure of program effectiveness.

Following the construction of the training program outline and objectives, and the initial design of the training program itself, the remaining objectives of this consulting project included: (1) conducting a pilot of the completed training program; (2) conducting a feedback session with the pilot's participants; (3) making any necessary revisions in the training program; (4) administering pretraining measure and conducting the training program for two hundred managers, in groups of twenty-five each; (5) administering posttraining measure; and (6) assessing the results of the training.

Since the previous report, the pilot program has been conducted, the feedback session completed, and the revisions have been made in the initial training program.

The pilot training program, held on May 10, was attended by twenty-three upper-level managers. The training program was conducted in much the same manner as it will be presented in final form. The program was eight hours long, with an hour break for lunch, and the training format combined facilitator lecture with video presentation and group and individual exercises.

On the following day, the same twenty-three upper-level managers met with me for eight hours to review the program and provide feedback and suggestions for necessary revisions. Each section of the training program was reviewed, comparing it to the stated objectives of the program. Both verbal and written feedback was obtained from the managers regarding what parts of that section were beneficial and what parts required revision. Suggestions for revisions and additions were also included in the participant's evaluations.

During the feedback session, it was noted that only six or seven of the participants gave consistent, meaningful feedback. However, the written portion of the evaluation generated substantive, valuable information from nearly all twenty-three participants. The suggested changes in training program outline and objectives, as well as in the program materials, have been derived from these evaluations. Due to the quality of the written evaluation in particular, I believe these suggested revisions reflect valid and reliable feedback from the pilot training program participants.

The strongest suggestion from the participants was that we expand the training program to two eight-hour days. The participants reported that they had sufficient time to complete the design of their own time management program by the end of the first day. However, the information on "Motivation, Procrastination, and Commitment" felt incomplete and rushed, they said. Also, the participants made several suggestions for additions to the program they felt would be beneficial, and that would provide several more hours to complete the second day of the two-day program.

Based upon this feedback, it was suggested that item #8 in the training program outline be completely revised and additional items included, and that several objectives for the training program be added as well. Thus, the following additions are proposed:

Training program outline:

8. Obstacles to Effective Time Management—Procrastination

9. Obstacles to Effective Time Management—Fears

10. Using Desire Motivation to Improve Time Management

11. Achieving Balance in All Areas of Life

Training program objectives:

7. Enhance effective time management by identifying pattern of procrastination, and constructing an Action Plan to overcome this pattern.

8. Enhance effective time management by identifying one's fear of success and fear of failure, and how they manifest themselves in destructive behavior.

9. Learn how desire motivation can best be implemented to improve one's management of time.

10. Identify the critical areas of one's live, and how to use time management techniques to achieve a healthy balance between these areas.

The necessary revisions in the training program have also been made, and are included at the end of this report for your approval.

It is recommended that we schedule a meeting as soon as possible to review these proposed revisions, and finalize them after you have approved them. We will also need to revise the training schedule, since the program will be two days long rather than one. We are currently on schedule to begin the training programs July 15 (see Training Program Timeline); however, with the implementation of the two-day program, the conclusion of the training programs will likely be in November or December, rather than the October 15 deadline initially scheduled.

Although the inclusion of a second day in the training program requires a substantive addition to the consulting project in terms of time and money invested, there are a number of benefits to consider. Among them are:

1. The material covered in the second day of training will further ensure that each participant succeeds in his or her time management program.

2. The additional information provided, for example, on procrastination, fear of success, etc., will assist the participants in becoming more effective in all areas of their professional lives, in addition to helping them manage their time.

3. The section on balancing all areas of life will help the participant improve his or her marriage and family life, which I understand is highly valued within your company.

4. Last, the inclusion of a second day allows a sense of team spirit and cooperation to emerge. This will help the participants implement their time management programs, as well as work together as a team on the job.

Open Communications

To effectively manage a consultant, you should have open communications and an open-door policy. The consultant should not feel that he or she cannot come to you with problems as they develop. Nor should the consultant feel you are going to view the adverse communications you receive as diminishing the work or

value of the consultant. Fundamentally, the point here is to get
the job done, and that requires a spirit of cooperation and open
communication, facilitating a system of early recognition of difficulties and problems.

Staff Member as Liaison

You should, if it is not going to be yourself, appoint a staff member as liaison between your organization and the consultant.
There should be at least one person, and preferably just one person, to whom the consultant can turn for clarification, to get
information, to set up appointments, to make arrangements, etc.
The liaison becomes a focal point in the organization, saving the
consultant a tremendous amount of time otherwise spent running
around trying to find the right person and dealing with interference from the political system of the client organization.

This appointed staff member should understand the objectives and purposes of the consultation and what the consultant
is aiming to accomplish. He or she should be familiar with the
political problems within the organization and with the seeming
threat the consultant poses to various people in the organization.

No matter what a consultant does, he or she is perceived by
some people in the organization as a threat. The consultant is a
strange character from outside, reminiscent of the days of efficiency experts with clipboard and stopwatch. Who knows what
the consultant is going to find? Who knows what the consultant
is going to see, or worse yet, what the consultant is going to say?
Many people do not like outsiders around, and these people will
sometimes throw up road blocks and interference. So a good internal liaison needs to recognize and understand these possibilities. He or she needs to be responsive to the consultant and to
educate the consultant about the problems in the organization.

Higher management must give this staff member sufficient
time to help the consultant if the consultation is going to be effective. You do not want to assign a person who already has too
much to do to be a liaison. If this added responsibility becomes
an undue, unappreciated burden on the staff member, he or she
will not cooperate with the consultant, and the consultant will
not be able to be effective.

Phased Payments

In most situations, you should not pay your consultant all of the money up front. Nor should you expect the consultant to have to wait until after the job is finished to get any money. You should phase the payment. Of course, if it is a very short consulting engagement, say, three days, the consultant can wait until the end of the week. But if it is a longer assignment continuing over several weeks or months, progress payments or phased payments—preferably tied to observable milestones—are the best and most equitable way to compensate a consultant. The consultant needs income, but you should not put yourself in a situation in which the consultant is paid in advance because the consultant may well lose motivation to get the job done when there is no longer motivation to collect money.

The smaller client with a short assignment may be required by the consultant to pay the entire fee up front as an advance retainer. The question of credit worthiness is the issue here. Fortune 500 firms (most of them anyway) need not worry about this, but the small consultant may need to.

Supportive Environment

Create an organizationally supportive environment for the consultant. An organizationally supportive environment suggests that the consultant and client are not hostile to each other; consultant and client are not adversaries, they are business associates, working together to produce the best possible result. This means that consultant and client do need a liaison, do need support, do need understanding, and do need open communications.

Quick Feedback

You should be able to provide quick feedback to the consultant about what is going right and what is going wrong. If you do not provide quick feedback, the consultant will continue down the wrong path for too long and may become committed to that path of work and reasoning. This is a part of open communications, but it also has to do with the speed with which communications take place. If there is a problem with the consultant's services, let him or her know quickly, and if you are satisfied with the way the consultant is working, communicate that as well.

Evaluating Yourself

The following is a checklist of questions to help you determine if you are doing your part to achieve the maximum potential of your consultant:

1. Did you set precise objectives?
2. Did you establish milestones?
3. Did you invest in needs analysis/confirmation of needs?
4. Did you buy only what you want and need in services—not what you don't want and don't need?
5. Do you avoid hidden agendas?
6. Did you prepare your staff?
7. Do you work with a written agreement?
8. Do you require progress reports?
9. Do you support your consultant, but delimit authority?
10. Do you retain decision-making authority and responsibility?
11. Do you remove bureaucratic and political barriers?
12. Do you foster communications?

Summary

There are certain measures you should take to facilitate a comfortable, productive, and mutually beneficial client-consultant relationship:

1. Set precise objectives for the project.
2. Establish observable milestones and a timetable.

3. Work with a written contract.

4. Use some form of progress report, preferably written.

5. Establish and maintain open communications.

6. Appoint a staff member as liaison between the client organization and the consultant.

7. Make phased payments.

8. Create a supportive environment.

9. Provide prompt feedback.

15
Ten "Should Have Communicated About" Issues

E xperienced buyers of consulting and professional services have, of course, learned lessons that will be of value to us. In a survey of 610 buyers of consulting/professional services, I discovered ten of the most frequently mentioned "should have communicated about" issues. These are outlined below, and the savvy client should not retain the services of a consultant without having clearly communicated about these issues (or having decided that they are inappropriate for the situation at hand).

Conflict of Interest/
Consultant Serving Your Competitor

The proper function of the consultant (and the only legitimate one) is to provide exclusive and sole attention to the client and his or her objectives. Consultants should never serve more than one master. That is, the consultant should place the client's interests ahead of any other interests, even the consultant's self-interest. Operationally, this often means that consultants should not, at least simultaneously, serve two clients in competition with each other. Further, it means that consultants should not be involved in situations that provide economic gain for themselves (other than the fee charged for services) through commissions, side deals, kickbacks, and so forth.

"Conflict of interest" is a unique subject because it is always determined through the eye of the beholder. Advertising agencies, as an example, normally operate on a policy of never serving two clients in the same business, even if the clients are in different markets. There is even one case with which I am familiar, where an agency spun-off personnel and created an entirely separate and autonomous agency to take care of a major airline account, while retaining a prior airline account in the original agency. On the other hand, it is somewhat common practice for certified public accountants to serve competitive clients, and who has more access to proprietary data than a CPA?

Thus, what might seem like a conflict of interest to one party may not seem so to another. This is clearly an area upon which you and your consultant must reach agreement.

The issue of kickbacks, commissions, referral fees, and the like is an issue that also must be aired. For example, suppose I know of two consultants who are both authorities on statistical analysis. Further, suppose that you are my client and that my responsibilities require the selection of such an expert for your project. Statistician consultant A charges a daily fee of $600, as does B. But, unknown to you, A pays me a commission or referral fee of 20 percent. Can I be sure that in recommending or referring A I have made the best selection for you, or have I made a selection influenced by my own monetary advantage? After all, you paid me a fee to make a decision that was in your best interest. I may not have served you well.

If the client is fully aware of the conflict, it is not nearly so bad or compromising a situation. And, if the consultant not only provides this awareness, but benefits the client from the conflict, such conflict may not be bad at all. I remember one consultation I conducted several years ago which, among other things, involved my selection of a piece of capital equipment for use in the client's business. Two months after installation of the equipment, I received from the equipment distributor an unexpected and unsolicited check of $500 along with a thank-you note for having specified their product. I did not even want to deposit this check into my account. I decided I had two options: one, return the check to the distributor, or two, endorse the check over to my client and let the client deposit it into his account. I chose the latter. This was an unexpected gain, and as I had already been paid a fee for my services in selecting this equipment, it made sense that my client should be the beneficiary.

Conflict of interest may also involve service to future clients in the same or similar industries as past clients. Just how long should a consultant wait until he or she markets his or her talents to others who are or may become other clients' competitors? Here again, you and your consultant must reach agreement. There are some clients who wish to limit the opportunity of their consultants to serve clients in the specific industry or market in perpetuity. Such a desire is understandable, but not realistic. In such a case, a consultant should include as a part of his or her fee the lost opportunity for future consulting. If one of my clients wished to withhold me in perpetuity from the marketplace, the idea might be fine, but I suspect that once the client learned of the cost of supporting me for the remainder of my working years, he or she might become far more realistic about the matter.

This discovery about the cost of withholding a consultant from the market usually makes the client more practical about what he or she really does not want the consultant to do, or really does not want the consultant to say to future clients. It is not so much a question of lack of discretion on the part of consultants, because they can be totally discreet; however, if a consultant spends two years working with you and learning all your proprietary procedures and processes, he or she cannot help but internalize those in his or her mind. Even if the consultant sets out never to communicate that confidential data to anyone else, eventually what information or ideas are yours and what are the consultant's will become blurred in the consultant's mind. So that is why clients, even with the most discreet consultants, worry about the conflict of interest when consultants serve their competitors.

Creative Outcomes

Ownership or right to use creative or proprietary results or technical data created during the consultation is another issue you and your consultant should discuss.

The law in most states says the client owns creative outcomes unless there is a specific agreement to the contrary. It comes under the "master and servant" statutes, which say that the work the servant does for the master belongs to the master. However, frequently consultants and clients agree to some other division of proprietary rights or data developed. If we create a patentable product or a copyrightable document, if we create a process or procedure which is useful and has commercial value, who owns it? Is it owned jointly, or by one party; if by one party, which party? This, too, is an area you and your consultant must explore and agree upon according to your specific needs and desires.

Associates and Subcontractors

Another issue clients say they wish they had communicated about is the consultant's use of associates or subcontractors in the completion of the assignment. Most clients do not mind if the consultant subcontracts part of the work, particularly to more qualified people—specialists in a given field. But it is something that should be discussed and agreed to, perhaps in the initial meeting, because you want to know, and should know, who is doing the work for you and who is in control. You should insist that even if work is subcontracted, it is the consultant who will take responsibility for the accuracy and suitability of work performed.

Time Management

The next issue that should have been discussed was time management. Schedules do slip; situations change. Clients change their desires; clients create problems for consultants that cause them to slow down, abandon schedule, or change the scope of work. Similarly, consultants sometimes find it takes longer than anticipated to get the job done. You should agree on how changes in the time schedule will be handled and on any financial penalties or incentives that might result.

Insurance/Liability

Most consultants automatically self-insure and limit the liability of the client from actions arising out of the work of the consultant, but this is something that should be confirmed. When I prepare a formal proposal or contract for my clients, it contains a statement of assurance that I will self-insure; I will hold my client blameless. Some 65 to 70 percent of consultants in this country put similar wording in the contract, but if it is not there, you ought to discuss this and make sure you are not becoming liable for actions or activities your consultant performs.

Termination

Contract termination should be discussed and treated in the contract in the event it should later become necessary. Who has the right to terminate? How much notice must be given? How is compensation to be handled? What situations give rise to or permit termination of the agreement? Without doubt, a termination clause should be discussed by client and consultant and included in the agreement.

Nonperformance

What happens if the consultant is unable to perform? Perhaps the consultant determines that he or she lacks suitable skills. Perhaps it is a result of events beyond the control of the consultant—death, disability; perhaps it is a result of other acts of nature and humankind—snowstorm, fire, earthquake, civil disobedience, war. Who then is liable? What is the extent of the liability? As rare as such occurrences may be, we would not want them to happen to you, and they should be, of course, included in the contract.

Arbitration

Because of the high cost of litigation and the long delay in adjudicating civil actions, more often today than in the past, consultants and clients are agreeing to binding arbitration in the event of a dispute. In binding arbitration, the normal procedure is for each party to select an arbitrator to represent its interests, and those two arbitrators in turn select a third arbitrator. There may be a definition as to who these arbitrators are or what kinds of people they may be. These three parties then arbitrate, and the client and consultant agree to live by whatever decision the arbitrators make. Often the parties do not like binding arbitration because by agreeing to it, they surrender their rights to seek redress in the courts. Matters such as these, and many others, should obviously be discussed with competent legal advisors.

Expenses

It is very often the case that clients wish they had talked to their consultants in more detail about the definition of expenses—what constitutes an expense?

If the agreement between consultant and client is on a fixed-price contract basis, the consultant pays for all expenses, and the client agrees to pay a fixed-price amount. But if it is a fixed-fee-plus-expenses or daily-rate-plus-expenses contract, it is useful to fully define what will constitute an expense for which the client is responsible. Was the consultant allowed to fly first class, or should the consultant only be compensated for having flown coach or at the least expensive discounted economy fare? Is the consultant allowed to stay at the finest hotel in town, or should the consultant stay at less expensive accommodations?

These are issues that should be decided before the consultation begins. Often you will find a consultant who is so professional and so conservative that these issues never arise. But do not take a chance that expenses might become an issue; instead, be able to ascertain that all possible problems are covered. If you are going to pay the consultant's expenses, define what expenses are and what amount of money can be spent.

Confidentiality

The last of our ten "should have communicated about" issues is confidentiality. This is not only confidentiality outside the organization, but within the client organization as well. Here, of course, we come full circle; not unlike conflict of interest, issues concerning confidentiality should be discussed openly and dealt with carefully and formally.

Summary

To prevent miscommunications, disagreements, and potential consulting disasters, there are ten issues client and consultant should discuss in clear, honest, and straightforward terms and make provisions for in their agreement or contract:

1. Conflict of interest
2. Creative outcomes
3. Associates and subcontractors
4. Time management
5. Insurance/liability
6. Termination
7. Nonperformance
8. Arbitration
9. Expenses
10. Confidentiality

Discussing and clarifying these issues in depth and providing for them in written agreement will certainly help ensure that the consultation is productive, beneficial, and successful for both client and consultant.

16
Evaluating the Consultation

The Final Report

Reporting the findings of results of the consultation is usually the culmination of the consultant's efforts and services on behalf of the client. The goal of the consultation is guidance and advice provided by the consultant to you, the client. Only if the final report gives the client guidance and understanding, and establishes conviction that its conclusions are correct and that the project is a success, can we say that the consultation has been effective.

An effective consultation results when the client receives that which he or she set out to achieve with the help of a consultant at a cost not dissimilar to the expected (or agreed upon) cost and in a time frame consistent with the time frame agreed upon at the beginning of the consultation. The final report can help to determine if these results have been achieved.

It is up to the client to decide whether a final report should be written, and in some cases a final report may not be essential—as in a very short-term, minor consultation. However, in almost all consultations, a report can be valuable and beneficial to the client and can serve several functions.

First, it brings the data, analyses, and findings into an organized and permanent form. It is often the only systematic source of documentation and will have to serve as a guide for further study, analysis, and research.

Second, the quality of the consultation is often judged by the quality of the report. This is particularly true when third persons not directly involved in the consultation will be making recommendations on the consultant's findings or evaluating the consultant's efforts.

Third, the effectiveness of the report may well determine the action taken by the client. After the consultation, the client must determine whether to implement the consultant's ideas—with or without the consultant's help. The written report can often give the client the best and clearest information about the consultant's advice and can help the client decide whether to act on the consultant's suggestions and exactly what action to take.

If you decide to require a final report, the report will be useless unless the consultant can present findings and conclusions in a fashion that communicates clearly and effectively to you, the reader. Content and presentation depend on who will be reading the report—what type of a client and organization you are. There are three general types of final reports: 1) technical reports, 2) reports for executives, and 3) reports for publication.

The Technical Report

The technical report is prepared for someone who requires detailed information about the procedures and results of the consultation. The reader of this type of report is usually someone with operational, technical, or middle management responsibility in the client organization. Besides giving detailed evidence that the project has been effective, this type of report helps the client with future decision making and long-range planning. It may lead to further analysis and study. The technical report gives in-depth treatment to the specific accomplishments and detailed methodology of the consultation.

The Report for Executives

The report for executives is designed to inform the reader of the crucial elements and findings of the consultation. It is usually intended for top-level decision-makers, such as CEOs and board members. These executives look forward to getting strong guidance for decision making, as well as demonstrated results that indicate the wisdom of having retained the consultant. Reports for executives are aimed both at giving a broad overview of the consulting project and providing information that can serve as the basis of decision making in the client organization.

The Report for Publication

The report for publication is the type most consultants prefer to make whenever possible. It disseminates the results and processes used during the consultation to an external audience. It is frequently recommended by consultants to clients for two reasons. First, the consultant's marketing advantage from a report for publication can be considerable, particularly when readers are likely to be potential clients themselves or when they may come in contact with potential clients. And second, although the report for publication requires greater creativity on the party of the consultant, it is often the easiest to write because of the relative absence of technical jargon, detailed explanations, and specific applications and recommendations the other types of reports require.

A given reporting effort often combines two or all three of these types. The most frequent combination is of an executive and a technical report; the executive report is prepared for top management, and the technical report is for middle management who will be in charge of implementing the consultant's findings. In addition, this type of combined report may be prepared for a party of interest, such as an outside auditor or evaluator. The information required by such external parties will likely differ from the needs of those within the client organization. For example, those who have provided funds for the project may be interested in how the funds were expended and whether the terms of the contract were met, while those within the client organization may have a need for more specific procedural data that will guide changes in approach or procedure.

Such dual reporting approaches allow high-level and external decision-makers to concentrate on major issues without being distracted by details, while making the more specific and detailed information available to those who need it.

The report for publication may be combined with either a

technical report or a report for executives. In either case, a report aimed at broadened readership both within and outside the client organization is accompanied by information specifically intended for the client or for those people who will assess the consultation.

The type of report should always reflect the interest of the client, regardless of what might benefit the consultant. For example, if a report for publication is much more beneficial for the consultant than the client, the consultant should never try to sell such a report to the client.

Requisites for the Written Report

Regardless of the type of report, all final written reports should include the following:

1. A statement of the goals and objectives of the consultation. These goals and objectives should be set out in terms that are as specific, measurable, and objective as possible.

2. An account of events that occurred during the project. The emphasis here is on events that helped to achieve the project's goals and objectives. Interesting but superfluous events should receive minimal discussion or be excluded entirely. Parts of the project that took a good deal of time and attention but were unproductive should also be left out, unless they are important because they represent avenues to be avoided in the future.

3. A discussion of the problems encountered and how they were overcome or resolved. The consultant should be honest about any difficulties that impeded the achievement of the project's objectives. If the consultant minimizes or glosses over such difficulties, you might well question the integrity of the consultant. It is important that the consultant discuss any problems so that the client organization can deal with them if they appear while implementing recommendations of if they recur in the future.

4. An examination of the results of the consulting project. This should be tied directly to the stated goals and objectives of the consultation, explaining to what extent these were achieved. Full explanations should be given as to why certain goals were met and why others were not.

5. Conclusions and recommendations for further implementation and/or study. Again, these should be an outgrowth of the goals and objectives of the project and the extent to which they were achieved.

When reviewing a final report, it may be helpful for you to keep these points in mind to help you assess the validity and quality of the report. There are also other factors that may be beneficial to look for in a report:

1. The report should be useful. It should be written to be used as a resource, rather than a mere volume to collect dust on a shelf. Its use as a resource is particularly crucial if it is a technical report.

2. The report should effectively communicate information to the reader. It should be well-written and without spelling or grammatical errors; it should be clear, concise, and direct, leaving no room for misinterpretation or misunderstanding.

3. The report should be interesting, encouraging the client to read all of it. It should not be a chore to read a final report, but it often is.

4. The report should be credible, without errors of fact or method. Statements should be backed up with supporting evidence. Factual errors or unsubstantiated claims could indicate errors in the consultant's work, not just in the report.

5. The content of the report should be consistent with the needs and expectations of the readers. Also, the content should match the level of technical expertise of the read-

ers. The consultant should avoid terminology that does not add meaning to what the report is trying to communicate and should avoid jargon whenever possible.

Distribution of the Final Report

The client should have ultimate control over the distribution of the final written report. You may wish to keep a technical report in particular out of circulation because of its confidential or proprietary nature. Or you may want to make copies available to those in the organization who will implement the recommendations or who will further analyze and research the findings. You may even favor a wide distribution of the report within the organization or field because of the project's success. If the report is for publication, the consultant should keep your needs in mind in distributing the report or in selecting a publication vehicle. What will happen to the final report after the consultant has presented it to you is certainly an issue you should discuss with the consultant.

Potential Benefits of the Final Report

The final report has potential benefits for both consultant and client. Of course, the benefits for you are the ones which most interest you; however, it is wise to understand why the consultant might wish to write a final report for his or her own benefit.

Potential Benefits for the Consultant

1. The report is a reminder of the consultant contributions and increases the probability of repeat and referral business.

2. The report may lead to the implementation of the consultant's ideas in other departments and/or organizations. This can lead to the client's retaining the consultant's services at a future date.

3. The quality of the consultation is often judged by the quality of the report. This is particularly true when third persons not directly involved in the consultation are in the position of making recommendations on the consultant's findings or evaluating his or her efforts. Thus, it may be in the consultant's interests to write the best possible report.

4. The effectiveness of communication in the report may well determine whether the client chooses to carry out the consultant's ideas and suggestions.

Potential Benefits for the Client

1. The report will provide written evidence that the assignment has been carried out. It shows that the consultation has been delivered and indicates the successful achievement of the client's objectives. On the other hand, it can also provide evidence that the project has not been satisfactorily carried out, allowing you to decide what action to take.

2. The report will formally document the consultant's conclusions and recommendations. This can help the client make decisions, carry out long-term planning, and take advantage of future opportunities to implement the consultant's suggestions.

3. The report is often the only systematic presentation of the data, analysis, and findings resulting from the consultation. As a result, the report can serve as a guide for further study, analysis, and research.

4. Dissemination of the report may produce a "spread effect" throughout the organization for the consultant's ideas. In case management or administration changes, the ideas and results of the consultation can continue to be implemented and to benefit the client organization.

5. A good report can demonstrate to upper management and to the client's colleagues the wisdom of having retained the consultant.

Evaluating

Overall, the final report can be an essential part of your evaluation of the consultant's work. In reviewing the consultation and the final report, you might do well to keep in mind a few simple questions, though, of course, you will have your own categories of evaluation and your own measurement of satisfaction.

- Do the consultant's recommendations in the final report fulfill your needs—the reason the consultant was retained—and successfully solve your problems?

- Are the solutions realistic, practical, and affordable? Was the client organization able or will it be able to implement the suggestions?

- Was the final report aimed to satisfy you, the client, and your needs, or was it an attempt to sell more or future consulting services?

And perhaps most important:

- Would you use the consultant again?

- Would you recommend the consultant's services to anyone?

- Are you happy and satisfied with the service you received and the results of the consultation?

Your answers to these questions and others you may have, and your feelings of satisfaction—or dissatisfaction—will determine your reaction to the consultation, what further action you will take (implementation of the consultant's recommendations if you are satisfied; rejection of the suggestions, search for a new consultant, legal action if possible or necessary, if you are dissatisfied), and how you and the consultant will part ways. Ideally, client and consultant will part amicably, mutually satisfied with the results of the consultation—client with the quality of services and successful results and consultant with having rendered useful services and receiving ample compensation.

17
Conclusion

Y ou are aware from reading this book that the use of consultants by business, government, and individuals is increasing. You have gained some understanding of the consulting process and have picked up some tips on how to make the working client-consultant relationship more effective and profitable for you. The following is a summary of essential points for you to review, keeping in mind your individual needs, desires, and circumstances.

Definition of a Consultant

A professional consultant is an individual or a firm with special knowledge, skills, and talent who makes needed expertise available to a client for a fee, rendering advice and often helping successfully implement that advice with and for the client.

Situations for Which
a Consultant's Services May Be Needed

1. Need for specialized expertise, talent, or skill
2. Need for an independent, unbiased, frank opinion
3. Need for temporary technical assistance
4. Business cash flow problems
5. Need for expertise in the acquisition of resources
6. Political/organizational problems
7. Regulation

8. Availability of funds
9. Saving key personnel
10. Training

Types of Consultants

1. Advisory vs. Operational

   Advisory consultants—do research, arrive at conclusions, make recommendations, but are not personally involved in implementation of recommendations.

   Operational consultants—implement recommendations as well as provide them.

2. Part-time vs. Full-time

3. Process vs. Functional

   Process consultants (generalists)—broad, expansive, and skills-oriented; take their skills into any organization, industry, environment.

   Functional consultants (specialists)—use their particular skills in very narrow, unique, specific environments.

4. Large Firm vs. Small Firm

5. Academic vs. Commercial

Outline of the Consulting Process

1. Marketing and public relations
2. Request for services/request to serve
3. Initial meeting—face-to-face selling
4. Analysis of needs/problem identification
5. Development of specific proposal
6. Modification and negotiation
7. Contract
8. Provision of services
9. Reporting and evaluation

Ways to Find Qualified Consultants

1. Define needs and objectives
2. Consultants come to you
3. Referrals
4. Reading/writing ads
5. Directories
6. Conducting your own research for the ideal consultant
7. Leading authorities
8. Trade and professional associations
9. Brokers

Evaluating the Potential Consultant

1. Conduct a personal interview—meet face-to-face. Interview more than one consultant.

2. Ask questions, listen to answers, assess the consultant's operating style and what he or she says.

3. Discuss desired outcomes and expectations of the consultation.

4. Establish measurable objectives.

5. Discuss business arrangements—the nature of the financial arrangements and contractual terms and conditions.

6. Ask about experience and references. Check the references.

Assess your feelings about and impressions of the consultant. If you are comfortable with the consultant and confident with his or her suitability and competence, ask for a written proposal. If you are not comfortable and confident, look for another consultant.

The Consultant's Fee and Its Components

Daily Billing Rate

1. Daily labor rate—a charge for the consultant's labor.

2. Overhead—the consultant's expense of being in business.

3. Profit—a percentage of the total of daily labor rate plus overhead.

Other Billing Rates:

1. Fixed-price: firm fixed-price, fixed-fee-plus-expenses, escalating fixed-price, incentive fixed-price, performance fixed-price, fixed-price with redetermination.

2. Time-and-material contracts.

3. Cost reimbursement contracts: the cost contract, cost-plus-fixed-fee, cost-plus-incentive-fee, cost-plus-award-fee.

4. Retainers

5. Performance/contingency contracts.

The Proposal

If, after the initial interview, your are convinced of the potential consultant's competence, you should ask for a written proposal. The proposal may be as formal or as informal as you, the client, require.

The formal proposal consists of the following (it can be tailored to suit your needs);

The Front Section: a letter of transmittal, the proposal cover, the proposal title page, an abstract, a table of contents, a statement of assurances, a statement of need, a statement of objectives.

The Main Section: a functional flow diagram depicting the entire scope of activities the consultant can perform for the client, a time-line for the project, and a written narrative explaining the results to be achieved by each activity in the FFD.

The Conclusion Section: evaluation plan and procedures, reporting and dissemination plan, consultation/project management and organization plan, consultation/project price or bid, consultation staff statement of capability.

The Contract

If you have found the right consultant to serve and suit you, you and the consultant need to negotiate a contract—preferably written, even if not formal.

The contract should be as clear, straightforward, and specific as possible to prevent misunderstanding and to ensure successful and satisfactory results for both client and consultant.

The contract should provide the following:

1. A time schedule for the completion of services.

2. A requirement for adequate insurance coverage.

3. A provision preventing the consultant or the client from assigning the contract or subcontracting a part of it without the written permission of the other.

4. A provision giving the client the right to terminate the agreement.

5. If needed or wanted, a provision that only competent personnel may perform or continue to perform work for the company, or a request that specific individuals perform the work.

6. Other provisions may include requirements that the consultants obtain any approvals required by government agencies, that the consultant maintain adequate records, that the consultant make periodic reports to the company, and so on.

Making the Client-Consultant Relationship Function Smoothly

1. Set precise objectives.

2. Establish observable milestones.

3. Work with some form of written contract as an agreement.

4. Require some form of progress reports, preferably written.

5. Maintain open communications between client and consultant.

6. If it is not going to be yourself, appoint a staff member as a liaison between organization and consultant.

7. Phase payments.

8. Create a supportive environment.

9. Provide quick feedback—handle problems as they come up and express satisfaction as well.

Issues to Discuss with the Consultant before the Assignment

 1. Conflict of interests
 2. Creative outcomes
 3. Associates and subcontractors
 4. Time management
 5. Insurance/liability
 6. Termination
 7. Nonperformance
 8. Arbitration
 9. Expenses
10. Confidentiality

Evaluating the Consultation

The Final Report

The final report serves three primary functions:

1. The assembled report brings data, analyses, and findings, into an organized and permanent form to work with.

2. The quality of the consultation is often judged by the quality of the report.

3. The effectiveness of the report may well determine the action taken by the client.

The final report should include the following:

1. A statement of the goals and objectives of the consultation.

2. An account of the events that occurred during the project.

3. A discussion of any problems and how they were overcome or resolved.

4. An examination of the results of the consulting project.

5. Conclusions and recommendations for further implementation and/or study.

In evaluating the final report and the overall consultation, keep in mind a few simple questions:

1. Do the consultant's recommendations in the final report fulfill your needs and solve your problems?

2. Are the solutions realistic, practical, and affordable?

3. Was the client organization able or will it be able to implement the suggestions?

4. Would you use the consultant again?

5. Would you recommend the consultant's services?

6. Are you happy and satisfied with the service you received and the results of the consultation?

As you have seen, there are definite benefits from using consultants. Consultants can provide special expertise and skills, state-of-the art knowledge, and technology the client organization lacks without the expense of hiring and training full-time employees. Consultants can also provide honest, objective opinions from outside the organization, outside of the problem; they can give a new or different perspective and insight on a situation. Consultants often offer the most economical, most productive, most innovative, and fastest means of solving a problem or fulfilling needs and desires.

However, risks and pitfalls to hiring consultants do exist. Even though they may often be the most economical way to solve a problem, consultants are expensive, and if you hire the wrong consultant you may waste a considerable amount of money without solving your problem. And even if you do hire the right consultant, his or her recommendations or suggestions may not necessarily be feasible. Moreover, bringing in an outsider can create suspicion or distrust within an organization, and although you can try to alleviate distrust and create a supportive atmosphere, you may not always be able to do so.

While retaining a consultant often is the wisest decision you can make to solve your problems and fulfill your needs, sometimes it simply is not. In particular, there are many very routine problems out there which businesses, organizations, and individuals encounter every day. Hiring a consultant to solve very ordinary problems or provide easily accessible information can be a waste of your time and money if the information you need can be found elsewhere, perhaps through information products—software, audio and video tapes, manuals, and other publications. Indeed, many consultants and/or other professionals provide such information products; thus, you receive the benefits of their wisdom without the high costs of a consultation. If your problem or situation is easily recognizable and fairly routine, you might do well to look into the many information products available; you can obtain them or information about them through public and university libraries, bookstores, catalogues, directories, and so forth. And by using such information materials for simple or routine needs, you can retain a consultant for the unique and important situations for which a consultant's outstanding expertise can be highly necessary, valuable, and fruitful.

I wish to leave you with one further general thought. The use of consultants can be extremely rewarding and can serve to magnify your effectiveness, but you will have to work hard, as with any endeavor, to ensure that such is the case. Approach your consultant in a spirit of cooperation and accept the responsibility of being at least 50 percent responsible for the success achieved. To be good, a consultant requires a good client.

Bibliography on Consulting

The following publications are sources of information for continuing study on consulting. Where possible and/or appropriate, the citations have been annotated.

Albert, Kenneth J. *How to Be Your Own Management Consultant.* McGraw-Hill, New York City. 1978. Hardback book, 207 pages. Written for the corporate executive who wishes to be his own consultant rather than retaining the services of an independent consultant, there is still some useful information for the consultant and some clever humor.

————. *How to Solve Business Problems: The Consultant's Approach to Business Problem Solving.* McGraw-Hill, New York City. 1983. Hardback book. Examines the author's approach to problem solution as a consultant. While the nature of problem solution advanced is not universal within the profession, the book is worth reading to examine one professional's approach.

Altman, Mary Ann, and Robert Weil. *Managing Your Accounting and Consulting Practice.* Matthew Bender.

American Consulting Engineers Council. *Public Relations Guide for Consulting Engineers.* American Consulting Engineers Council, Washington, D.C. 1982.

Arnoudse, Ouellette and Whalen. *Consulting Skills for Information Professionals.* Dow Jones-Irwin. 1989.

Barcus III, and Wilkinson. *Handbook of Management Consulting Services.* McGraw-Hill. 1986.

Bavier, Ralph. *How to Break 100 in the Consulting Game.* Kennedy and Kennedy, Fitzwilliam, NH. Pocket-size softback and 23-minute cassette. Describes how his firm made list of one hundred top consulting firms. Rambling, anecdotal, but often inspirational.

Bell, Chip, and Leonard Nadler. *Clients and Consultants.* Second edition. Gulf Publishing, Houston, TX. 1979.

Bermont, Hubert, James L. Kennedy, and Howard L. Shenson. *Bermont, Kennedy, Shenson Consulting Conference, The.* Howard L. Shenson, Woodland Hills, CA. 1980. Live audio recording of consulting conference with written materials.

Bermont, Hubert. *Complete Consultant, The: A Roadmap to Success.* Consultants Library, Sarasota, FL. 1982. Hardcover book, 125 pages. Reprints of a monthly opinion letter on the consulting profession once published by the author. More Bermont philosophy, well-written, interesting, often humorous.

————. *Consultant's Malpractice Avoidance Manual, The.* Second Edition. Consultants Library, Sarasota, FL. 1986. Softcover book, 23 pages. A basic introduction to the issue of malpractice in consulting. Useful background reading but not sufficiently authoritative to be comprehensive on the subject.

————. *Consultant's U.S. Statistical Guide and Source Finder, The.* Consultants Library, Sarasota, FL. 1986. Softcover book, 57 pages. Book contains a bibliography listing sixty-three books on consulting, addresses of thirty-three publishers of the sixty-three, names and addresses for fifty-three consulting professional associations and five newsletter publishers, reprint of a 1985 study on the economics of the consulting profession (a more recent study is available elsewhere), names and addresses of nine organizations offering courses/seminars on consulting and of thirty-five computer software packages the author views as useful for consultants.

————. *How to Become a Successful Consultant in Your Own Field.* Second edition. Consultants Library, Sarasota, FL. 1985. Hardcover book, 148 pages. The first edition was a well-written and interesting autobiography on how the author began his own consulting practice. The second edition has been enhanced by including the bulk of some of the author's other books, but it is still not a comprehensive, generally applicable manual on building a practice. The book provides excellent philosophical background reading for the new consultant.

————. *Psychological Strategies for Success in Consulting.* Consultants Library, Sarasota, FL. 1982. Softcover book, 72 pages. Pop psychology and more Bermont philosophy on consulting.

————. *Successful Consultant's Guide to Winning Government Contracts, The* Consultants Library, Sarasota, FL. 1981. Softcover book, 122 pages. Some very basic information on government contracts plus a list of agencies that procure the federal government.

————. *Successful Consultant's Guide to Writing Proposals and Reports, The.* Consultants Library, Sarasota, FL. 1979. Softcover book, 51 pages. Easy and quick-to-read overview for the novice consultant, but not all the techniques advanced are generally in use by consultants.

Bigood, Reginald. *Future Markets for Consultancy.* Northwood Books, Institute Press, Midland, MI. 1981.

Block, Peter. *Flawless Consulting*. Learning Concepts.

Boen and Zahn. *The Human Side of Statistical Consulting*. Lifetime Learning, Belmont, CA. 1982.

Burgher, Peter H. *Professional Excellence*. Agness Press.

Cody, Thomas. *Management Consulting: A Game without Chips*. Consultants News. Fitzwilliam, NH. 1986. Focuses on some of the long-term issues and problems facing management consultants, deals with the changing role of management consultants, and includes the author's thoughts on how clients will be required to change to maximize their benefit from using consultants.

Coe, Charles K. *Consulting Engineer: Getting the Most from Professional Services*. University of Georgia Press, Athens, GA. 1979.

Cohen, Stanley. *Consulting Engineering Practice Manual*. McGraw-Hill, New York City. 1981.

Cohen, William A. *How to Make It Big as a Consultant*. AMACOM, New York City.

Communications Consultant. Jobson Publishing Corporation, New York City. Monthly magazine on consulting in voice, data, and image consulting. Many articles are specific to communication but a number of articles would apply to consultants regardless of field of specialization.

Computer Consultant, The. Seniority Magazine, Inc., Syracuse, NY. Monthly tabloid with articles on the computer business. Articles on consulting practice and use of consultants are frequent and some apply to consultants outside of the computer field.

Connor, Richard A., Jr., and Jeffrey P. Davidson. *Marketing Your Consulting and Professional Services*. John Wiley and Sons, Inc., New York City.

Conoley, Jane C. *Consultation in Schools: Theory, Research, Procedures*. Academic Press, New York City. 1981.

Consultants News. Kennedy and Kennedy, Fitzwilliam, NH. Monthly newsletter oriented toward large firms and management consulting. Provides information on management consulting and personnel changes in larger firms. Oldest newsletter published for the management consulting profession.

———. *Fee and Expense Policies/Statements of 24 Management Consulting Firms*. Kennedy and Kennedy, Fitzwilliam, NH. Some examples of boilerplate that may be helpful in insuring profitability, avoiding losses, and resolution of client/consultant disputes. Includes information on fees, payments, expenses, and limits on liability.

———. *How Much Is a Consulting Firm Worth?* Kennedy and Kennedy, Fitzwilliam, NH. 1983. Small but powerful potpourri of ideas, formulas, case histories, and reprints on determining the value of a management consulting firm. Includes a checklist of fifteen factors for determining value.

———. *Future of Management Consulting, The*. Kennedy and Kennedy,

Fitzwilliam, NH. Opinions, representing all of management consulting's constituencies, on trends, growth areas, and implications of future. Includes 72-minute cassette outlining views of management consulting association's spokespersons.

————. *News Release Idea Book for Management Consulting Firms.* Kennedy and Kennedy, Fitzwilliam, NH. 1983. Ring bound, 290 pages, includes 25-minute introductory audio cassette. Contains scores of news releases sent out by management consulting firms.

————. *Thoughts on Profit Centers in Management Consulting Firms.* Kennedy and Kennedy, Fitzwilliam, NH. 1982. Results of an informal study of fifteen larger firms, more conceptual and philosophical than statistical, though it does contain some data on percentages, margins, assessments, allocations, and chargebacks.

————. *25 Best Proposals by Management Consulting Firms.* Kennedy and Kennedy, Fitzwilliam, NH. 1984. A twenty-page introductory text accompanies examples of proposals for management consultants.

————. *What Clients Really Think about Consultants: 160-Turn-ons & 163 Turn-offs in 4 Phases of the Engagement.* Kennedy and Kennedy, Fitzwilliam, NH. Reactions from fifty-five clients and prospects—some perceptions "obvious," yet frequently ignored.

Consulting Opportunities Journal. Consultants National Resource Center, Gapland, MD. Bimonthly newsletter. Reasonably well-written articles and reprints from other publications on consulting in general. Useful for the beginning consultant as well as those with limited professional experience.

————. *How to Successfully Market Your Professional Consulting Practice.* Consultants National Resource Center, Clear Spring, MD. Six short reports by J. Stephen Lanning, et al., on starting and building a consulting practice. Of particular value to the new consultant.

Easton, Thomas A., and Ralph W. Conant. *Using Consultants.* Probus.

English and Steffy. *Educational Consulting: A Guidebook for Practitioners.* Educational Technical Publications, Englewood Cliffs, NJ. 1984.

Executive Recruiter News, The. Kennedy and Kennedy, Fitzwilliam, NH. Monthly newsletter. Companion newsletter to publisher's other letter, *Consultant's News,* but directed toward search firms.

Fordyce Letter, The. The Kimberly Organization, Des Perese, MO. Monthly newsletter. Largest circulation, most widely quoted newsletter in the executive search field.

Fuchs, Jerome H. *Making the Most of Management Consulting Services.* American Management Association, New York City. 1975. Hardcover book, 214 pages. A classic, written from the vantage of the buyer of consulting services. Somewhat outdated, but still useful reading.

———. *Management Consultants in Action.* Hawthorne Books, Inc., New York City. 1975. Hardcover book, 216 pages. A classic with some very useful advice, even if somewhat dated.

Garrison, Guy. *Changing Role of State Library Consultants, The.* University of Illinois Press, Champaign, IL. 1968.

Garvin, Andrew P. and Hubert Bermont. *How to Win with Information: Or Lose without It.* Consultants Library, Sarasota, FL. 1980. Hardcover book, 171 pages. Well-written and useful book on how to take advantage of the flood of information now available for consultants and others, a field that is moving so rapidly that some of the data are less than current.

Gleeck, Fred. *Consultants Manaual.* Growth Resources, Inc., Boca Raton, FL. 1986. Author has borrowed extensively from other publications, to create yet another version of a how-to manual. Most useful to the novice who has not read some of the many publications available.

———. *How to Start and Build a Consulting Practice in Your Own Field.* Growth Resources, Inc., Boca Raton, FL. Six audio cassette tapes and 50 pages of written materials. Information from other seminars on building a consulting practice. Author adds a few new interesting ideas.

———. *Marketing Public Seminars.* Growth Resources, Inc., Boca Raton, Fl. 1986. Three hours of audio cassettes with some written material. Largely a replay of information published by others.

———. *Selling Consulting Services.* Growth Resources, Inc., Boca Raton, FL. 1986. Live recording of half-day seminar on audio cassettes with some written materials. This Gleeck publication contains the most new and original material of the four he markets. Though there is liberal borrowing from other works on selling and marketing consulting services, Gleeck's primary expertise is in sales and there are some good insights from his unique experience.

Golightly, Henry. *Consultants: Selecting, Using and Evaluating Business Consultants.* Watts.

Good, Bill. *Selling Consulting Services.* Howard L. Shenson, 1980. Eight audio cassette tapes (6½ hours) plus written materials. An excellent professional selling program directed specifically at the selling environment encountered by consultants and other professional practitioners.

Goodryder, Ernest. *How to Earn Money as a Consultant.* Business Psychology International, Boston. 1978.

Gowan, Vincent Q. *Consulting to Government.* Infoscan Ltd., Cambridge, MA. 1979. Hardcover book, 368 pages. Comprehensive and useful reading but the reader should be advised that the book has a distinct Canadian as well as large-firm orientation.

Gray, Douglas. *Start and Run a Profitable Consulting Business.* Self Counsel Press, Seattle, 1984.

Greiner, Larry E. and Robert O. Metzger. *Consulting to Management.*

Prentice-Hall, Englewood Cliffs, NJ. 1982. Hardcover book, 361 pages. An excellent book, well-written and particularly of value to management consultants.

Hameroff, Eugene and Sandra Nichols. *How to Guarantee Professional Success: 715 Tested, Proven Techniques for Promoting Your Practice.* Consultants Library, Sarasota, FL. 1983. Hardcover book, 183 pages. Excellent idea-generating book on marketing of consultant services, useful for the experienced and new consultant.

Harper, Malcolm. *Consultancy for Small Businesses.* Intermediate Technology, Croton-on-Hudson, NY. 1983.

Higdon, Hal. *Business Healers, The.* Random House, New York City. 1969. Hardcover book, 337 pages. Author is a free-lance writer who describes his views on the consulting profession in the late 1960s.

Holtz, Herman. *Advice, a High Profit Business. A Guide for Consultants and Other Entrepreneurs.* Prentice-Hall. 1986.

———. *The Consultant's Guide to Newsletter Profits.* Down Jones-Irwin. 1987.

———. *How to Become a More Successful Consultant with Your Personal Computer.* Consultants Library, Sarasota, FL. 1985. Continuing a trend of writing on hot topics, Holtz has combined his knowledge of personal computers and consultants to develop this interesting, even if not highly authoritative, work.

———. *How to Succeed as an Independent Consultant.* John Wiley and Sons, New York City. 1983. Hardcover book, 395 pages. Well-written and much useful information.

———. *Successful Newsletter Publishing for the Consultant.* Consultants Library, Sarasota, FL. 1983. Hardcover, 130 pages. Well-written introduction to the newsletter business.

———. *Utilizing Consultants Successfully: A Guide for Management in Business, Government, the Arts, and Professions.* Greenwood Press, Westport, CT. 1985. Holtz has written numerous books on a wide variety of subjects including consulting. As with many authors, he recognized in the early 1980s that there might be a demand for a book on how to use consultants. This is his contribution to that area, but it is written from the vantage of a practicing consultant/author.

Hunt, Alfred. *Management Consultant.* John Wiley and Sons, New York City. 1977.

Johnson, Barbara. *Private Consulting: How to Turn Experience into Employment Dollars.* Prentice-Hall, Englewood Cliffs, NJ. 1982.

Kelley, Robert E. *Consulting: The Complete Guide to a Profitable Career.* Charles Scribners and Sons, New York City. 1981.

Kelley, Kate. *How to Set Your Fees and Get Them.* Visibility Press.

Kennedy, James H. *Public Relations for Management Consultants.* Kennedy and Kennedy, Fitzwilliam, NH. 1979. Softcover book, 83 pages. A collection of articles by Kennedy and others written for the management consultant but useful for consultants regardless of field of specialization.

Kirby, Jonell H. *Consultation: The Practice for the Practitioner.* Accelerated Development, Muncie, IN. 1984.

Kotler, Philip, and Paul N. Bloom. *Marketing Professional Services.* Prentice-Hall, Englewood Cliffs, NJ. Kotler is a well-known authority on marketing and this book is considered a modern classic for the professional practitioner regardless of field of specialization.

Kubr, M. *Management Consulting: A Guide to the Profession.* International Labour Office, Switzerland. 1982. Hardcover book, 368 pages. Well-written; large-firm and European orientation.

Kuecken, John A. *Starting and Managing Your Own Engineering Practice.* Van Nostrand Reinhold, New York City. 1978.

Lant, Jeffrey L. *Consultant's Kit, The: Establishing and Operating Your Successful Consulting Business.* Second edition. JLA Publication, Cambridge, MA. 1982. Oversize softcover, 201 pages. Well-written and interesting, but somewhat difficult reading for the beginner.

———. *Money Talks: The Complete Guide to Creating a Profitable Workshop or Seminar in Any Field.* JLA Publications, Cambridge, MA. 1985. The book is more comprehensive with respect to building a paid speaking business than with respect to doing seminars and workshops. Lant is bright and has a great deal of experience, making the book good reading.

———. *Tricks of the Trade: The Complete Guide to Succeeding in the Advice Business.* JLA Publications, Cambridge, MA. 1986. Oversize softcover, 316 pages. The most recent of Lant's books. In a sense, a follow-on to his earlier work on consulting and reflects some of the reasoning in Lant's thinking that has resulted from his experience in the recent past.

———. *Unabashed Self-Promoter's Guide, The.* JLA Publications, Cambridge, MA. 1983. Oversize softcover, 366 pages. Type style and language usage make the book somewhat difficult to read, but it is full of highly useful information, often humorous, and an outstanding resource for those who wish to conduct their own public relations campaign regardless of occupation or profession. Since the author is a consultant, many of the examples will be of value to professionals in the field.

Levoy, Robert P. *Successful Professional Practice.* Prentice-Hall, New York City. 1970.

Marcus, Bruce. *Competing For Clients.* Probus.

Maris, Terry L. *Management Consulting.* Reston, VA. 1985.

McGonagle, John J. Jr. *Managing the Consultant: A Corporate Guide.* Chilton.

Merry and Allerhand. *Developing Teams and Organizations: A Practical Handbook for Managers and Consultants.* Addison Wesley, Reading, MA. 1977.

Moore, Gerald L. *The Politics of Management Consultants.* Praeger, New York City. 1984.

Murphy, Harry. *Grantsmanship Consulting.* Howard L. Shenson, Woodland Hills, CA. 1981. Eight audio cassettes (6½ hours) plus written materials. A detailed and sophisticated course for those consultants who wish to obtain government and foundation/corporate grants to finance consulting projects. Such grants may be obtained directly or on behalf of clients.

Niland and Emory. *Productivity through Consulting in Small Industrial Enterprises.* Unipub, New York City. 1974.

Nugent, John W. *The Singleton Markets His Services.* La Cresta Publications, Palos Verdes, CA. 1979. Oversize softcover, 104 pages. Good book for the novice that describes some useful marketing techniques.

O'Malia, Thomas. *How to Find Money.* Howard L. Shenson, Woodland Hills, CA. 1980. Complete unabridged seminar on audio cassettes including manual. Covers the intricacies of the banking game.

Pilon, Daniel H., and William H. Bergquist. *Consultation in Higher Education.* Council for Advancement of Small Colleges, Washington, DC. 1979. Oversize softcover, 159 pages. Excellent book, particularly for those consultants working in the higher education field.

Poynter, Dan. *The Expert Witness Handbook.* Para Publishing Santa Barbara, CA. 1987.

Professional Consultant and Information Marketing Report, The. Howard L. Shenson, Woodland Hills, CA. Monthly newsletter. Largest circulation newsletter in the consulting field, continuous publication since 1977. Includes how-to articles as well as news and economic statistics/surveys on the profession.

Pyeatt, Nancy. *Consultant's Legal Guide, The.* Consultants Library, Sarasota, FL. 1980. Hardcover, 145 pages. A basic but useful introduction to the consultant's legal environment. Appropriate for the novice consultant in particular.

Schein, Edgar H. *Process Consultation: Its Role in Organization Development.* Addison Wesley, Reading, MA. 1969. A classic book on the behavioral science process.

Seiden and Matthiew. *Breaking Away. The Engineer's Guide to a Successful Consulting Practice.* Prentice-Hall. 1987.

Shenson, Howard L., CMC. *Advanced Consulting Seminar, The.* Howard L. Shenson, Woodland Hills, CA. 1980. Live recording and written materials from an advanced seminar on marketing of consulting services.

————. *Beyond Consulting: Information Entrepreneurship.* Howard L. Shenson, Woodland Hills, CA. 1987. Live recording and written materials from a seminar on how to develop and market information products and services.

—. *Complete Guide to Consulting Success.* Enterprise Publishing, Wilmington, DE. 1989. 247 page, tab-divided, three-ring-bound manual. Comprehensive, how-to manual on building and maintaining a profitable consulting practice, appropriate for the sophisticated beginner and established professional.

—. *Consultant and Productization, The.* Howard L. Shenson, Woodland Hills, CA. 1981. Audio recording and written material on developing information products from one's consulting expertise and experience.

—. *Consultant's Guide to Proposal Writing, The.* Howard L. Shenson, Woodland Hills, CA. 1982. Oversize softcover book, 206 pages. Written for both the experienced and new consultant. Provides detailed, how-to strategies on preparation of professional consulting proposals in both formal proposal and letter-style format. Only comprehensive work known to be available that deals with the unique attributes of consulting proposals. Contains sample proposals.

—. *Consulting Handbook, The.* Fifth Edition. Howard L. Shenson, Woodland Hills, CA. 1982. Oversize softcover, 209 pages. Written for both experienced and new consultants as a resource guide on consulting. Regarded by many as "the encyclopedia of consulting." Covers a broad range of topics on consulting but must be regarded as strategic and not basic.

—. *Economics of Consulting: 1980–1990, The.* Howard L. Shenson, Woodland Hills, CA. 1981. Audio cassette and written material on the economic environment of consulting for the decade of the 1980s.

—. *How to Build and Maintain Your Own Part-time/Full-time Consulting Practice.* Audio I. Howard L. Shenson, Woodland Hills, CA. 1985. Three audio cassettes (4½ hours) plus 78 pages of written materials. Developed for both experienced and new consultants. Concentrates on marketing of consulting services. Strategic in orientation. Live, unabridged recording of seminar.

—. *How to Build and Maintain Your Own Part-time/Full-time Consulting Practice.* Audio II. Howard L. Shenson, Woodland Hills, CA. 1985. Eight audio cassettes (6¼ hours) plus 204 pages of written materials. A more detailed and strategic presentation of a live recorded seminar that concentrates on marketing and strategic factors relevant to building a profitable consulting practice.

—. *How to Build a Profitable Consulting Practice.* Volumes I and II. Chesney Communications. 1988. Two one-hour + professional quality videos. Volume I features consulting opportunities and marketing strategies and Volume II discusses proposal writing, contracting, fees, and collections.

—. *How to Buy a Business with No Money Down.* Howard L. Shenson, Woodland Hills, CA. 1988. Live, unabridged, professional recording of the seminar comes complete with the full manual and copies of visuals used in the seminar.

—. *How to Create and Market a Successful Seminar or Workshop.*

Consultants Library, Sarasota, FL. 1987. Softcover book, 108 pages. Written for the experienced and new consultant or trainer as well as those in the seminar business on the subject of successful marketing of open-enrollment seminars and workshops.

———. *How to Develop and Promote Profitable and Successful Seminars and Workshops.* Audio I. Howard L. Shenson, Woodland Hills, CA. 1984. Six audio cassette tapes (6 hours) plus 81 pages of written materials. Developed for both consultants and trainers and concentrates on the marketing of public seminars and workshops as well as captive, contract training programs. Live, unabridged recording of seminar.

———. *How to Develop and Promote Profitable and Successful Seminars and Workshops.* Audio II. Howard L. Shenson, Woodland Hills, CA. 1985. Eight audio cassettes (6½ hours) plus 204 pages of written materials. A more detailed and sophisticated version of the Audio I program.

———. *How to Select, Manage, and Compensate Consultants, Trainers, and Professional Practitioners.* Howard L. Shenson, Woodland Hills, CA. 1984. Written primarily for buyers of consulting and professional services, but highly useful information for the consultant as well. Based on research with more than six hundred clients regarding likes, dislikes, preferences, expectations, etc.

———. *How to Start and Promote Your Own Newsletter for Profit and/or Personal Image Building.* Howard L. Shenson, Woodland Hills, CA. 1985. Three audio cassette tapes (3¼ hours) with written materials. Developed for the experienced and new consultant. Provides a complete turnkey program for starting, promoting, and managing a successful newsletter. Useful for those wishing to enter newslettering on a for profit basis as well as those who wish to use a newsletter only for building image and reputation. Live recording of seminar.

———. *How to Strategically Negotiate the Consulting Contract.* Revised, Third Edition. Howard L. Shenson, Woodland Hills, CA. 1986. Softcover, 119 pages. Written for both the experienced and new consultant, the newly revised book contains eleven example contracts as well as a strategy guide for developing and negotiating the consultant's contract. The book is also available on computer disk for both IBM-PC/compatibles and Apple Macintosh in several different versions compatible with word processing software that allows the user to combine, add to, and modify the sample agreements directly on word processing equipment without the need to first type the text in the book.

———. *Marketing Your Professional Services.* Howard L. Shenson, Woodland Hills, CA. 1985. Six audio cassette tapes (6 hours). Developed for the experienced consultant and professional practitioner as an advanced program on marketing strategies such as referral business, advertising, image building, face-to-face sales meetings, and related topics. Live recording of six one-hour lectures.

———. *Research Reports.* Howard L. Shenson, Woodland Hills, CA. 1989.

Twenty-two different research reports on consulting, seminar and information marketing and consulting practice management.

——. *Successful Consultant's Guide to Fee Setting, The.* Consultants Library, Sarasota, FL. 1986. Softcover book, 71 pages. Written for both the experienced and new consultant, the book contains complete information on calculating overhead rates, determining fees, alternative methods of disclosing the fee to the client, and reimbursement for direct expenses.

——. *Strategic Seminar and Workshop Marketing.* Howard L. Shenson, Woodland Hills, CA. 1985. Results of a number of field research studies, including data analysis on topics such as selecting seminar topics, determining program profitability potential, site selection, comparisons of promotional methods, when to engage in promotional activities, etc.

Shenson, Howard L., CMC, and Rafferty, Gerald. *Publishing Is Your Second Business.* Howard L. Shenson, Woodland Hills, CA. 1987 Strategic, unabridged, professional recording of the live seminar by Howard L. Shenson and author/publishing executive Gerald Rafferty comes complete with full manual.

Shenson, Howard L., CMC, and Joseph Schachter. *Marketing Consulting Services.* Howard L. Shenson, Woodland Hills, CA. 1980. Audio cassette tapes (3 hours), book, and worksheets. Assists reader to plan and develop a consulting practice, identify market strengths/niches and engage in direct promotional efforts.

Shenson, Howard L., CMC, and Dottie Walters. *How Consultants Can Build a Lucrative Paid Speaking Business.* Howard L. Shenson, Woodland Hills, CA. Three audio cassette tapes (3½ hours). Developed for experienced and new consultants. Live recording of seminar. Deals with the development, marketing and management of a consultant's paid speaking business.

Sinha, Dhorni P. *Consultants and Consulting Styles.* MCB Publishing. 1980.

Slavin, William E. *How to Start and Manage a Computer Consulting Practice.* Home Enterprises Unlimited, Sierra Madre, CA. 1983. Two audio tapes. An interview of Slavin by Paul and Sarah Edwards. Particularly appropriate for the beginner or an individual considering starting a consulting practice in the computer area.

Smith, Brian R. *Country Consultant, The.* Kennedy and Kennedy, Fitzwilliam, NH. 1982. Hardcover book, 300 pages. Useful book for the solo consultant, particularly those who will practice in a rural environment.

Spiro, Herbert T. *Financial Planning for the Independent Professional.* John Wiley and Sons, New York City. 1978. Hardcover book, 235 pages.

Steele, Fritz. *Consulting for Organizational Change.* University of Massachusetts Press, Amherst, MA. 1975. Hardcover book, 202 pages. Interesting reading on the consulting process.

——. *Role of the Internal Consultant, The: Effective Role-Shaping for Staff Positions.* Van Nostrand Reinhold, New York City. 1982.

Stryker, Steven C. *Guide to Successful Consulting with Forms, Letters, and Checklists.* Prentice Hall, Englewood Cliffs, NJ. 1984.

———. *Principles and Practices of Professionalism in Consulting.* Consultants Library, Sarasota, FL. 1982. Hardcover, 145 pages. Well-documented and research, scholarly book on consulting practice, but not easy reading—it reads like a college text.

Thomsett, Michael C. *Fundamentals of Bookkeeping and Accounting for the Successful Consultant.* Consultants Library, Sarasota, FL. 1980. Hardcover, book, 136 pages. A very basic bookkeeping/fundamental accounting course applied to the consulting practice. Useful for someone with little or no knowledge of basic accounting.

Tisdale, Patricia. *Agents of Change: The Development and Practice of Management Consultancy.* W. Heineman, distributed by David & Charles, North Pomfret, VT. 1983.

Tomczak, Steven P. *Consulting Reports 1-6.* Steven P. Tomczak and Associates, 1978. Six oversize softcovers 28 to 46 pages in length. Basic reading for the novice consultant. Monographs have an engineering consulting orientation.

Wilson, Aubrey. *Marketing of Professional Services, The.* McGraw-Hill, New York City. 1972. Hardback book, 193 pages. This work is considered a classic and has some meaningful applications for the consultant in today's environment.

———. *Practice Development for Professional Firms.* McGraw-Hill, New York City.

Wolf, William B. *Management and Consulting: An Introduction to James O. McKinsey.* Industrial and Labor Relations Division, Cornell University Press, Ithaca, NY. 1979.

Unipub. *Guide for Drawing Up International Contracts on Consulting Engineering, Including Some Related Aspects of Technical Assistance.* Unipub, Xerox Corporation, New York City. 1983.

Index

About the Author

Howard L. Shenson began part-time consulting in 1969, while serving in administrative and teaching capacities at the University of Southern California and The California State University.

After three years, he resigned his position as chair of the management faculty at California State University, Northridge to enter full-time consulting.

Shenson is a Certified Management Consultant who specializes in the marketing of consulting and professional practices and information products and services, including seminars, publications, and software. His clients include major corporations, small businesses, not-for-profit organizations, government agencies, and universities, as well as individual entrepreneurs, consultants, professional practitioners, authors, and speakers.

Shenson has written more than three dozen books, audio/video packages, behavioral instruments, and software programs, and is the editor of his own newsletter, *The Professional Consultant and Information Marketing Report,* which has been in continuous publication since 1977. He has been active in forming and developing associations within the profession and has written numerous journal and magazine articles and monographs.

He is a frequent speaker before national and regional professional and trade associations. More than one hundred thousand people have attended his seminars on marketing consulting and professional practices, seminar promotion, entrepreneurship, and information product/service development and marketing. His seminars have been sponsored by prominent universities, professional societies, and commercial entities.

He is frequently consulted by the press for his interpretation of events related to his areas of specialty. He has been the subject of more than four hundred newspaper and magazine articles and has participated in more than 250 radio and television talk and news shows.

Shenson maintains offices in the Los Angeles suburb of Woodland Hills and lives with his wife and three sons in Calabasas, thirty miles northwest of downtown Los Angeles.